# PREPARED TO PREACH

This short book contains a wealth of powerful and practical wisdom for the preacher. Whether you are an occasional preacher, an experienced pastor-teacher, or working through a growing sense of calling to preach, you will find this book extremely helpful. The key note that Scharf strikes throughout is preparation: first the preparation of the preacher, and second, the preparation of the message. This right biblical balance is a timely reminder of the seriousness of the task. Preaching is not mere explanation – it is proclamation of the living and enduring Word of God. In the detailed chapters on preparing the message Scharf excels. His careful and logical approach will surely result in better preaching – there is no higher commendation for a book on preaching.

**Rev. Robin Sydserff**
**Minister, St Catherine's Argyle Church**
**Edinburgh, Scotland**

# PREPARED**TO** PREACH

## GOD'S WORK & OURS IN PROCLAIMING HIS WORD

# GREG**SCHARF**

**ⅢENTOR**

Greg Scharf studied biology at Rice University where he came to realize he was a sinner and turned to Jesus as his Savior. He earned M.Div. and D.Min. degrees from Trinity Evangelical Divinity School where God convinced him of the key role of the local church in His eternal plan.

Dr Scharf served at All Souls, Langham Place in London, England and Knox Church, Toronto, Ontario before moving to Fargo, North Dakota to pastor Salem Evangelical Free Church for 19 years. He has ministered the Word in a variety of settings around the world.

Dr Scharf is Associate Professor and Chair of the department of Pastoral Theology at Trinity Evangelical Divinity School in Deerfield, Illinois, USA. He has served as president of the Evangelical Homiletics Society and is an active member of Arlington Heights Evangelical Free Church.

All Scripture quotations, unless otherwise indicated, are taken from the *Holy Bible, New International Version®*. NIV®. Copyright ©1973, 1978, 1984 by International Bible Society. Used by permission of Zondervan. All rights reserved.

Scripture quotations marked ESV are from *The Holy Bible, English Standard Version*, copyright © 2001 by Crossway Bibles, a division of Good News Publishers. Used by permission. All rights reserved."

ISBN 1-84550-043-1
ISBN 978-1-84550-043-6

Published in 2005
Reprinted 2007 and 2010
in the
Mentor Imprint
by
Christian Focus Publications Ltd.,
Geanies House, Fearn, Ross-shire,
IV20 1TW, Scotland
www.christianfocus.com

Cover design by Alister MacInnes

Printed by
Bell & Bain, Glasgow

Mixed Sources
Product group from well-managed forests and other controlled sources
www.fsc.org Cert no. TT-COC-002769
© 1996 Forest Stewardship Council

# Contents

## Epilogue

# Preface

This book will be more helpful to you if your expectations of it correspond to those of its author. As I write, I have in mind a reader who is already motivated to learn to preach, who perhaps has done some preaching, and who has been challenged to preach or feels a growing compulsion to do so. I am assuming that your time is limited because preaching is not the only thing you do. You may indeed be a pastor-teacher, or aspire to that role, but I write also for the parachurch worker who speaks from the Bible to students, the short-term missionary who anticipates being asked to preach, the layperson who is occasionally asked to preach or who wants to be able to give a clear devotional message or Bible talk, and the student who wants to grasp the basics of preaching. Many books have been written about preaching that go into more depth than this one and are written by people whose training and experience equip them to consider various angles of preaching. I will recommend a number of these books as we go along. I am indebted to their authors for virtually all the ideas you will find here.[1] You may have already read some of these books; if so, this exercise will be a review. Since most who pick up this little book won't have read other books on preaching, I won't assume that you use the jargon, or care about the technical matters that concern homileticians (those who study preaching). Instead, I attempt to lay out in a few words how you can prepare to preach.

---

[1]Bryan Chapell, *Christ-Centered Preaching: Redeeming the Expository Sermon* (Grand Rapids: Baker, 1994); Haddon Robinson, *Biblical Preaching: The Development and Delivery of Expository Messages,* 2nd ed. (Grand Rapids: Baker Academic, 2001); John Stott, *Between Two Worlds: The Art of Preaching in the Twentieth Century* (Grand Rapids: Eerdmans, 1982); and Peter Adam, *Speaking God's Words: A Practical Theology of Expository Preaching* (Downers Grove: InterVarsity, 1996) have been especially formative. Lloyd Perry, John Stott, and Michael Bullmore taught me a great deal in classes, and John Stott also did so by example for the years I served at All Souls in London.

I hope you won't use this book merely as a 'how-to' manual, offering a list of tips, things you can *do* in order to preach. That would be a misguided understanding of preaching and would grant to the preacher entirely too much prominence in the process. There are indeed a number of things you, the preacher, must do, but these are not at the heart of preaching. It is what God does that is at the heart of preaching.

My prayer is that these words will be used by the Triune God to assist in equipping preachers whose messages are faithful to Scripture, clearly expressed (and therefore understandable), sensitive to the situation, and anointed by the Holy Spirit. When God's people hear his voice and obey, the church will be built up, God will be glorified, and the powers in the heavenly realms will marvel at his multifaceted wisdom that he could stoop to use people like us to make a name for himself (Eph. 3:10).

I am grateful to the Regents of Trinity Evangelical Divinity School for allowing me a sabbatical in the spring of 2004 to work on this project and especially to colleagues Don Carson, Steve Roy, Mike Bullmore, Gene Swanstrom, Dana Harris, and Ken Langley for their valuable feedback and candid suggestions, many of which I was able to implement. Several students read a draft of the manuscript. Among them, Jonathan Menn's detailed critique was especially helpful. I appreciated Dr. Kent Hughes, my pastor, Colin Smith and David Jackman for taking time to read the manuscript and offer encouragement. My son Graham helped with some computing issues and made valuable comments on the manuscript, and the whole family offered timely encouragement although my wife Ruth is, as always, peerless in that respect. Naturally, despite all the helpful suggestions, I take responsibility for the final product. To these people, and those who pray for me regularly or occasionally, and to the One to whom they pray, I express my sincere thanks.

# Part One

# Preparing to Prepare

# 1

## What Is Preaching?

If we begin by assuming that preaching is merely what preachers do, we will almost certainly distort the preparation process. We will be tempted to work only on the knowledge, attitudes, and skills we as preachers need in order to preach. Instead, let us recall some basic assertions of Scripture that will point us in another direction.[1]

**God speaks.** Sometimes he speaks directly. As early as Genesis 1:3, even before humans were present, God spoke and there was light. When God speaks, he speaks clearly, truly, purposefully, authoritatively, and sufficiently. He speaks to be heard. He speaks to be obeyed.

**God also speaks through means.** Not all of his speech thunders directly from heaven. God speaks, for instance, through creation (Ps. 19:1-4). God speaks through his messengers, angels (Luke 2:10-12). God speaks through prophets who are, as it were, his *mouth*, as Aaron was to Moses (Exod. 7:1-2). Ultimately, God speaks through his Son, the exact representation of his being (Heb. 1:1-3). His speaking through these means does not diminish his word in any way. It is to be heeded, even though it is mediated.

**God spoke his *written* word.** He breathed out the whole of Scripture, the sixty-six canonical books of the Old and New Testaments (2 Tim. 3:16-17). As a result, men 'spoke from God as they were carried along by the Holy Spirit' (2 Pet. 1:20-21). Yet the Bible is not merely the product of this process, nor simply a deposit of truth, though it is certainly that. 'The word of God is living and active. Sharper than any two-edged sword, it penetrates even to dividing soul and spirit, joints and marrow; it judges the thoughts and attitudes of the heart' (Heb. 4:12).

---

[1]See Peter Adam, *Speaking God's Words* (Downers Grove: Intervarsity, 1996) and *Hearing God's Words: Exploring Biblical Spirituality* (Downers Grove: InterVarsity, 2004) for a fuller development of these ideas.

**God still speaks through his written word.** He speaks through us when we speak from his written word in his name and by his power. Paul and his coworkers were deeply encouraged when they preached to the Thessalonians that the gospel came to their listeners not merely as words but with power, the Holy Spirit, and deep conviction so that the gospel in turn went forth from them (1 Thess. 1:4-8). They thanked God, saying 'when you [Thessalonians] received the word of God, *which you heard from us*, you accepted it not as the word of men, but as it actually is, the word of God which is at work in you who believe' (1 Thess. 2:13). Additionally, 'If anyone speaks, he should do it as one speaking the very words of God' (1 Pet. 4:11). The word *should* in 1 Peter 4:11 and the apostolic elation over the Thessalonians imply that those who speak sometimes fail to speak as oracles of God and their listeners do not always receive what they say as what it actually is, the word of God. So our understanding of preaching will necessarily be an ideal, a goal toward which we strive.

Instead, then, of thinking of preaching as what we do with God's word, we are wiser to think of it as what God does with his word through us.[2] After all, Paul could write that 'Scripture ... preached the gospel beforehand to Abraham' (Gal. 3:8 ESV). So how do we define 'preaching'? John Stott captures the essence of it: 'To preach is to open up the inspired text with such faithfulness and sensitivity that God's voice is heard and God's people obey.'[3] We preach the Word when our messages have the right source, the right content, the right immediate purpose, and the right ultimate goal.

Our *source* is the Word of God to which every message is faithful. The preacher expounds a text, a unit of thought from the Bible, or some appropriate collection of biblical texts. The Bible in its various parts and as a whole sets our agenda. Its literary genres

---

[2] J. I. Packer says, 'Christian preaching is the event of God himself bringing to an audience a Bible-based, Christ-related, life-impacting message of instruction and direction through the words of a spokesperson.' *Preaching the Living Word: Addresses from the Evangelical Ministry Assembly* (Fearn, Scotland: Mentor/Christian Focus Publications, 1999), 28.

[3] Personal conversation, February, 2003.

shape our messages, its tone sets our tone, its truths are what we preach, its authority gives us boldness, and its permanence gives us relevance in every age. Peter captures it well when he describes the Bible as the enduring word of God, the word of the Lord which stands forever. 'And this is the word that was preached to you' (1 Pet. 1:23-25).

Our sermon's *content* is truth from God that the Bible teaches. Whether it is sound doctrine to believe, an example to follow or avoid, a command to obey, or a warning to heed, the subject of the sermon corresponds with the subject that the passage addresses. These are the things we 'teach and urge' (see 1 Tim. 6:3).

Our *immediate purposes* in preaching are in keeping with the purposes of our text in its context. Ultimately every part of the Bible points to Christ (Luke 24:25-27), and was given to make us wise for salvation through faith in him (2 Tim. 3:15). All Jesus taught his apostles is written so that we may use it to make disciples who obey all his commands (Matt. 28:20). But not all texts are commands. A passage may play another role. It may be designed by the Holy Spirit to encourage, instruct, or rebuke, for instance. The preacher discovers that role and urges listeners to respond in ways consonant with it.

The *ultimate goal* of our preaching is the glory of God. God is pleased and glorified when our listeners receive the Word of God for what it is and respond in faith, hope, and love as the Thessalonians did. Such a hearing is possible only when the Holy Spirit opens blind eyes and illuminates the word. The Word sanctifies believers who then reflect the nature of God (John 17:17). God is glorified – though in a very different way – when people harden their hearts and close their ears. His holiness and righteousness are seen, in that case, not because rebellious people reflect his nature, but because they prove his word true, his character unchanging, and his judgments just. (Consider, for instance, Isaiah 6 and 29 and how they find fulfillment in 1 Corinthians 1:18-2:5.)

To preach the Word, then, is to declare in his name and by his power, from one or more texts of the Bible, what God placed there in order to achieve his ends for his glory. Or to put it negatively, we fail as preachers when any source other than the Bible supplies our message, when our sermon's thrust fails to respect the thrust of the text, or when our aims, either immediate or ultimate, are contrary to the text's purposes. When we fail in any of these ways we have not given voice to God's word. We must let God's voice be heard in the assembly and among the nations. 'Preach the Word!' (2 Tim. 4:2).

# 2

# God Prepares Preachers

You are preparing to preach. That is good. But it would be a serious mistake to think that God would leave the preparation of preachers to the preachers themselves. The message we are given to preach is so important, the church is so greatly loved, and the lengths to which God has already gone to rescue humanity are so great, that he has not risked this link in the chain by leaving it entirely in our hands. We have vital responsibilities, but the task of preparing preachers begins with God himself. As we have already seen, God is unwaveringly committed to getting his word out to his world. Creation itself declares God's glory.

> The heavens declare the glory of God;
> the skies proclaim the work of his hands.
> Day after day they pour forth speech;
> night after night they display knowledge.
> There is no speech or language where their voice is not heard.
> Their voice goes out into all the earth,
> their words to the ends of the world (Ps. 19:1-4a).

God's message, even when mediated by creation, is plain: 'For since the creation of the world God's invisible qualities – his eternal power and divine nature – have been clearly seen, being understood from what has been made, so that men are without excuse' (Rom. 1:20). He still uses creation, and if need be, would give voice to beasts and rocks (cf. Luke 19:40; Num. 22:21-41). He has countless messengers called angels to whom he could entrust his message. On occasion he speaks directly to people by means of dreams and visions. But as history unfolded, God saw fit to speak through prophets, who were to speak to his people as his own mouth, speaking his word so it could be obeyed. Moses, the prototype of all the prophets, said that God spoke to the people face to face when he, Moses, spoke: 'I stood between the LORD and you to declare to you the word of the LORD because you were afraid of the fire and did not go up the mountain' (Deut. 5:4-5). The prophets prepared the way for the Father's definitive word, his unique Son, the *incarnate* Word. 'In the past God spoke to our forefathers through the prophets at many times and in various ways, but in these last days he has spoken to us by his Son, whom he appointed heir of all things and through whom he made the universe' (Heb. 1:1-2). His life, death, resurrection and ascension, his gift of the Holy Spirit, together with the promise of his return, created the gospel, the good news we preach. Just before his ascension he opened the minds of his followers to understand the Scriptures, charged them to preach repentance and forgiveness of sins in his name to all the nations, and promised the presence and power of the Holy Spirit to clothe them (Luke 24:45-49).

How has God manifested his commitment to getting his message to the nations in the days since Pentecost? We can learn from three means: (1) what God said when he called prophets, (2) Christ's promises to the apostles, and (3) the record of the earliest church. Remember that God does similar things for all who minister in his name, not just those who preach. Here we notice what he does to prepare preachers.

## God makes preachers

Jeremiah said, 'The word of the LORD came to me, saying, "Before I formed you in the womb I knew you, before you were born I set you apart; I appointed you as a prophet to the nations"' (Jer. 1:5). God created Moses who described himself as 'slow of speech and slow of tongue' (Exod. 4:10). Timothy was timid and sensitive (2 Tim. 1:7). The apostle Paul was a highly-trained, zealous rabbi (Acts 22:3). Peter was an unlettered fisherman (Acts 4:13). God does not have only one template for preachers. He created our minds and mouths and gave them to us to declare his praises. He sovereignly superintends our whole lives, weaving together parentage, personal experiences, formal and informal education, and personality to make preachers. Whether by strengths or weaknesses, he suits us to speak for him (2 Cor. 12:7-10).

## God regenerates preachers

The apostle Paul understands that birth is not enough; there must be rebirth. 'But when God, who set me apart from birth and called me by his grace, was pleased to reveal his Son in me so that I might preach him among the Gentiles, I did not consult any man' (Gal. 1:15-16). For Paul to be qualified to preach, God had to pour out his grace on him, along with the faith and love that are in Christ Jesus (1 Tim. 1:14; see also Eph. 3:7). No doubt there have been preachers who have *not* been God's children, but their fraudulent character underscores the necessity that true preachers be those who actually know the One in whose name they speak. Paul's aspiration to preach was subservient to his aspiration to know the Christ who apprehended him on the road to Damascus. We would do well to follow his example.

## God calls preachers

Although the word *call* has a range of meanings in Scripture, I use it here to underscore the fact that God will let you know that you are being prepared and authorized to preach. What the writer to the Hebrews says of high priests is true of preachers, 'No one takes this honor upon himself; he must be called by God, just as Aaron was' (Heb. 5:4). But how do we know we are called to preach? Sometimes the call to preach is dramatic. Saul, the persecutor of the church, encountered the risen Christ on the Damascus road, heard his voice, and was blinded by the light. It took another miracle to restore his sight. Ananias, whom Christ instructed in a vision to lay hands on Saul that he might see again, was afraid to have contact with the notorious persecutor of the church. Jesus said to Ananias, 'Go! This man is my chosen instrument to carry my name before the Gentiles' (Acts 9:15; Gal. 1:15-16). Once Saul received his sight, was filled with the Holy Spirit, and was baptized, he began to preach in the synagogues. Paul's conversion and call to preach were intertwined.

More often a call to preach is the sum total of all the things God does to prepare us. Somehow or another, God will make it clear that you must preach. It may be that a truth of Scripture speaks to you as you carefully study it or hear it preached. It may be mainly an inner inclination, a longing or aspiration to preach, a word from someone that is neither flattery nor manipulation but provides some confirmation to you that you should preach. Because such experiences are subjective and personal, you will want to make sure that you do not take your stand on them, like some in Colosse who were puffed up with idle notions, their carnal minds inflated with what they had seen (Col. 2:18). God who stooped to give Gideon a sign knows how to help all of us be confident that he does indeed want us to preach. If you *lack* this inner sense of God's call to preach, ask him to give you the assurance that you need. Don't be surprised if he answers you in terms of the more verifiable confirmation that we will discuss shortly. If you *have* this inner assurance, make sure that you do not trust *it* apart from the other indications he gives. Paul could speak of himself as being *commissioned* by God to serve the church (Col. 1:25), *appointed* as a herald (1 Tim. 2:7), and *approved* by God to be *entrusted* with the gospel (1 Thess. 2:4). Jesus himself appointed Paul to be a servant and a witness of what he had seen and would be shown (Acts 26:16). Paul *knew* that he was authorized to serve as an apostle. That was crucial in light of his pivotal role and the resistance he faced. Yet when his protégé, Timothy, was selected for church leadership, the call was apparently mediated and confirmed through others.[1] What then are these other, more public assurances God gives?

## God gifts preachers

Every Christian has at least one spiritual gift. Though they may have other gifts, those who oversee the church *must* be 'apt to teach'.[2] The spiritual gift creates the aptitude, building in some cases upon a talent that is also God-given. So important is this that one of the four kinds of gifted individuals that God gives to the church

---

[1] 1 Timothy 1:18; 4:14. See also Acts 16:2. Timothy is the only postapostolic church leader whose selection is described in the New Testament.

[2] 1 Timothy 3:2. Titus 1:9 expands this aptitude, requiring that elders be able to 'encourage others by sound doctrine and refute those who oppose it'.

to equip it for ministry is the pastor-teacher.[3] He also gives to others teaching and preaching gifts. Teaching and preaching are both ministries of the word. There is significant overlap in the semantic range of the words *teaching* and *preaching* in the New Testament. *Teaching* emphasizes providing instruction and emphasizes the *content* of what is taught. *Preaching* builds on this foundation of patient instruction (2 Tim. 4:2) and urges 'acceptance and compliance'.[4] Gifts are given so that the body of Christ, the church, might be built up. If you have teaching gifts, use them, stir them up, and fan them into flame (2 Tim. 1:6). People will grow; the body will be built up. If you don't have teaching gifts, it does not follow that you will not have a ministry; only that you will not have a *teaching* ministry. Don't mistake the God-given call to serve within the body of Christ with the God-given prompting to preach. The two are not identical. By his body and Spirit, God will equip and gift you for ministry, but not necessarily the ministry of the word through preaching.

### God equips preachers

Spiritual gifts are necessary for preachers but not sufficient. Everyone in the body of Christ is to be equipped for ministry, including those such as pastor-teachers who equip others. God does this through the church. The church equips saints for preaching by teaching them sound doctrine, and how to live it, study it, explain it, and apply it. This book was written to help equip preachers.

### God affirms preachers through the church

In the church in Antioch there were five men who were *recognized* as prophets and teachers (Acts 13:1). When Apollos wanted to minister in Achaia, 'the brothers encouraged him and wrote to the disciples there to welcome him' (Acts 18:27). They recognized his

---

[3]Ephesians 4:11. The use of the word for 'some' in the original links the two functions into a single office.

[4]Johannes P. Louw and Eugene A. Nida, eds., *Greek-English Lexicon of the New Testament Based on Semantic Domains*, 2nd ed. (New York: United Bible Societies, 1989), 417.

gifts and equipping and how teachable he was. Paul routinely commended the character and dedication of members of his teams and others in the churches he planted.[5] He did not hesitate to warn Timothy about those who could *not* be trusted (2 Tim. 4:9, 14-15). Paul himself was affirmed by the pillars of the Jerusalem church who saw that God was at work in his ministry and that God's grace was upon him. They specifically recognized that the gospel had been entrusted to him for the Gentiles (Gal. 2:7-10). If God wants you to preach, others whom the church recognizes as seasoned leaders will see it. That is why it is crucial to use your gifts in the context of a local church where recognized leaders and others can affirm your ministry and thank God for the fruit it bears. Their recommendations safeguard the church from those who aspire to preach but have not been sent by God to do so.

## God empowers preachers by his Holy Spirit

When Peter preached at Cornelius' house, he described Jesus as anointed with the Holy Spirit and power. When the apostles preached they knew similar power. Sometimes that preaching was confirmed with signs and wonders.[6] However, these were not what commended the gospel in Thessalonica. There Paul reasoned from the Scriptures with those in the local synagogue, 'explaining and proving that Christ had to suffer and rise from the dead' (Acts 17:2). He described the same events later saying that the gospel came to them with power, the Holy Spirit, and deep conviction. Paul and his coworkers knew it had done so because they saw faith, hope, and love in these new converts. Others saw it too. The Thessalonian church became a model to other churches. In other words, the Thessalonians 'received the preaching not as the word of men, but as it actually is, the word of God' (1 Thess. 1:2-10; 2:13). Moreover, Paul's understanding of the Spirit's ministry both freed him from reliance upon his own 'eloquence or superior wisdom'

---

[5] See for instance, 1 Corinthians 16:12-18; Philippians 2:19-30; and Colossians 4:7-15.

[6] See Acts 2:43; 4:30; 5:12; 8:13; 14:3. These reflect Old Testament examples (Acts 7:36) and the ministry of Jesus (Acts 2:22).

(1 Cor. 2:1) and gave him the right kind of confidence, since he knew his competence came from God (2 Cor. 3:4-6). God does not let his word languish for want of his power. Those whom God calls to preach will experience this kind of power in preaching. (Read 1 Samuel 3:19–4:1a for an encouraging example of this fact.)

### God deploys preachers in answer to prayer

The Lord Jesus invited his apostles to ask the Lord of the harvest to send out workers into his harvest field. The problem is that workers are few compared to the size of the harvest (Matt. 9:35-38). Therefore, it is crucial that the Lord himself deploy, according to his wisdom, in answer to prayer, *all* the workers he has made, regenerated, called, gifted, equipped, affirmed, and empowered. The fewness of workers and the abundance of the harvest dictate that deployment must not be left to the inclinations of the workers. It is the Lord who sees the whole field and who knows where each unique worker should serve. These assignments are not merely cross-cultural ones. Nor are they communicated to the preacher in isolation from the church. Acts 13:1-3 records how God deployed Saul and Barnabas to locations other than Antioch. The Holy Spirit spoke to those who were worshipping the Lord and fasting, 'Set apart for me Barnabas and Saul for the work to which I have called them.' After they fasted and prayed, they laid hands on Barnabas and Saul, and the two of them were 'sent on their way by the Holy Spirit' (Acts 13:4). Preachers do not just go, they are sent (Rom. 10:15). They are sent by the Lord when we ask him to do so. They are sent by the Holy Spirit who is at work in the church.

### God gives words to preachers

God reached out his hand and touched Jeremiah's mouth and said, 'Now, I have put my words in your mouth.' That act elevated Jeremiah above the nations (Jer. 1:9-10). When Philip preached in Samaria, and the apostles in Jerusalem heard of the faith of his listeners, they referred to it as accepting the word of God.[7] To

---

[7] Acts 8:4-14. The same expression is used when the first Gentiles responded. See also Acts 11:1; 12:24; 13:7; and 17:13. The phrase 'the

be sure, the genuine Old Testament prophets and the New Testament apostles were in a category by themselves. What *they* spoke stands written as Scripture. What *we* speak derives from Scripture and must always be tested by it (1 Cor. 14:29; 1 Thess. 5:21). We cannot claim divine inspiration for everything we say when we preach. Nevertheless Peter exhorts *anyone* whose gift is speaking 'to do it as one speaking the very words of God'.[8] In Scripture God has given us the words to speak. We are to speak as those who have his words, read them publicly and speak from them in ways that let God's authentic voice sound forth. It is, to use Paul's phrases in 2 Corinthians 5:20, 'as though God were making his appeal through us. We implore you on Christ's behalf.'[9] Jesus promised the seventy-two, (not just the twelve), 'The one who hears you hears me' (Luke 10:16 ESV). His voice is heard when we preach his word for his purposes.

---

word of the Lord' describes what the listeners wanted to hear in Acts 13:44, what they honored in 13:48, and what spread in verse 49. Paul and Barnabas regarded the places they had evangelized in their missionary journey as 'the towns where we preached the word of the Lord' (Acts 15:36). See also Acts 19:10, 20.

[8] 1 Peter 4:11. The plural word that is used here, *lōgia*, which is sometimes translated 'oracles', is found three other times in the New Testament (Acts 7:38, Rom. 3:2, and Heb. 5:12). In the first instance, Moses received living words to pass on to others. In the second, the chief advantage of the Jews was that to them had been entrusted the oracles of God, i.e., God's words. In the third passage, it could stand for the sayings of God or be a collective for Scripture from which the readers should already have learned the basics of the faith. In all three cases, people received God's word in oral or written form. The Christian preacher's assignment is to speak so that the sermon communicates God's truth and comes with God's authority.

[9] Peter Adam in *Hearing God's Words*, 179-202, describes how Quaker views (in the 1650s) elevated the immediately apprehended internal word (perceived as coming from the Spirit) that then replaced the objective written word, Scripture. Though we want to underscore the prominence God has given to preaching, we do not want to exalt what preachers say in ways that ultimately undermine the written word that enables them to speak as God's oracles.

## God accompanies preachers

Having gone to these lengths to get his message into the hearts of people, God does not send out preachers only to abandon them. When God called Samuel, 'the Lord was with Samuel as he grew up and let none of his words fall to the ground.... And Samuel's word came to all Israel' (1 Sam. 3:19-4:1a). When God gave words to Moses for the Israelites standing before Sinai, he said, 'I am going to come to you in a dense cloud so that the people will hear me speaking with you and will always put their trust in you' (Exod. 19:9). God wanted to elevate confidence in his messenger by making sure the listeners knew where the words ultimately came from. Indeed so awesome was God's presence that they begged Moses to speak and promised to listen (Exod. 19:16; 20:18-19). When God called Jeremiah he watched to see that his word was fulfilled (Jer. 1:12). Listen to the challenge and encouragement of his commission to Jeremiah:

> Get yourself ready! Stand up and say to them whatever I command you. Do not be terrified by them, or I will terrify you before them. Today I have made you a fortified city, and iron pillar and a bronze wall to stand against the whole land – against the kings of Judah, its officials, its priests and the people of the land. They will fight against you but will not overcome you, for *I am with you* and will rescue you (Jer. 1:7-19).

In Corinth, Paul had God's commitment reaffirmed to him in a vision. 'Do not be afraid; keep on speaking, do not be silent. For I am with you and no one is going to attack and harm you, because I have many people in this city' (Acts 18:9-10). Even without a vision such as Paul had, we can count on God's presence. Our Lord Jesus, armed with all authority, explicitly promises his presence with those who go to make disciples, baptizing and teaching the nations to obey all he commanded. That promise is good to the end of the age (Matt. 28:18-20).

Since God has gone to these lengths, two things follow: he will hold us accountable for all he has given us, and he will get the glory when the word achieves its purposes. When his word – proclaimed by his redeemed creature, who is gifted and empowered by his Spirit, deployed by his Son, affirmed by his church, and accompanied by his presence – bears fruit, it is only right that he get the glory. The fact that he holds us accountable is a reminder that we must still prepare.

# 3

## We Who Preach Still Need to Prepare

If you aspire to preach I suspect you will have read these words of Jesus.

> You must be on your guard. You will be handed over to the local councils and flogged in the synagogues. On account of me you will stand before governors and kings as witnesses to them. And the gospel must first be preached to all nations. Whenever you are arrested and brought to trial, do not worry beforehand about what to say. Just say whatever is given you at the time, for it is not you speaking, but the Holy Spirit.[1]

Having just seen how God is so actively involved in preparing preachers, this saying of Jesus may simply confirm the conviction that God does it all, that we do nothing, that preparation to preach is unnecessary. But remember, Jesus offered this promise to his followers in the hour of their persecution, not for their regular teaching. We, too, may be taken before religious or civil authorities. Under arrest and facing trial, we can count on the Holy Spirit to give us the words to say just when we need them. We are not to worry or be anxious concerning either what we say or how to say it.[2] That part of the command and promise has a wider application. We need not *worry* about what to say when we preach because normally we have the time to *think* about what to say and to *pray* about it. When we do that and humbly submit to the Bible, study it carefully, and meditate upon it, its message becomes clear to us, clear enough to preach. When we trust God – whatever the circumstances – he will give us what we need to speak for him. When there is time, he gives it to us through reverent study; when there is not, he gives it more directly. In neither case is worry warranted. Jesus prohibits not preparation but worry. He both commands and gives faith. He promises that the Holy Spirit *will* speak through us.

---

[1] Mark 13:9-11. See similar instructions in Matthew 10:19; Luke 12:11-12; 21:14-15.

[2] See parallel in Matthew 10:19.

What shall we make of the apparent absence of *preparation* to preach in the book of Acts? It is true that Luke does not say much about preachers preparing sermons, nor, for that matter, about people preparing meals. Jesus had invited his followers to ask our heavenly Father to give them daily bread. Did this mean they did not have to earn money to buy flour or take time to bake bread? No – the silence of the Acts of the Apostles about preparation proves nothing. Some things are assumed. Furthermore, Acts is an inspired account of historical events. It is essentially *descriptive* rather than *prescriptive*. Even if preparation were absent, we would still have to ask whether that feature is an example to follow or simply an accurate report of how things happened immediately after Pentecost. In short, we would need indications from the text itself that the example is normative or at least exemplary of something other texts of Scripture clearly teach. Most of the proclamation that Luke records in Acts is the initial proclamation of the good news. That proclamation mainly involved testimony, bearing witness.[3] By its very nature, *testimony*, when true, is fundamentally not something one prepares. The witness just reports what he or she has seen or heard.

Nevertheless, Luke *does* mention preparation for preaching, even if indirectly. The whole church from the very beginning devoted themselves to the apostles' teaching (Acts 2:42). *Everyone* was engaged in intentional feeding on what Luke calls *the teaching*. This is the most basic and indispensable preparation for preaching. So, later, when the apostles gave attention to prayer and devoted themselves to the ministry of the word, it seems reasonable to assume that they did not try to minister what they did not study, ponder, and consider how to expound (Acts 6:4). That ministry of the word was more than testifying to the word; it was also proclaiming,[4] teaching,[5]

---

[3]See Acts 4:20; 5:32; 10:42; 14:3; 20:21, 24; 22:15, for instance.

[4]*Katangellō* is used in Acts of proclaiming the resurrection through Jesus (4:2), and through him the forgiveness of sins (13:38), of proclaiming Jesus (17:3), God (17:23), the word of God (13:5; 15:36; 17:13), the way to be saved (16:17), and light to Jews and Gentiles (26:23). *Kērussō* is used of announcing or heralding Christ (8:5), that Jesus is the Son of God (9:20), of the Jesus that Paul preaches (19:13), and of the kingdom (20:25; 28:31). Preaching is linked to testifying in 10:42. *Euangelizomai* means to proclaim good news and is

and reasoning from Scripture.[6] The apostle Paul manifested a similar focus when Silas and Timothy joined him in Corinth. 'Paul was occupied with the word, testifying to the Jews that the Christ was Jesus' (Acts 18:5 ESV). Surely this absorption with the word was not merely with speaking it but also with reading it, feeding upon it, pondering it, and thinking how its parts connected and how he could reason and persuade others with it. Once churches were planted, the ministry of the word tended to emphasize teaching, establishing, and encouragement (Acts 11:26; 13:1; 14:21-22; 20:2).

Early on, the apostles were considered unlettered men whose power derived from having been with Jesus (Acts 4:13). Later, Apollos is approvingly described as 'a learned man, powerful in the Scriptures'. God was evidently doing something in him that involved his active participation in learning. He was prepared. Nor should we fail to notice that he was teachable.

> He had been instructed in the way of the Lord, and he spoke with great fervor and taught about Jesus accurately, though he knew only the baptism of John. He began to speak boldly in the synagogue. When Priscilla and Aquila heard him, they invited him to their home and explained to him the way of God more adequately (Acts 18:25-26).

Apollos's ability to preach with growing accuracy was linked to his having been instructed and his willingness to keep learning.

Paul was certainly a reader, including the writings of Cretan prophets and Greek poets.[7] All the while he was self-consciously

---

sometimes used absolutely in that way (14:7, 21, etc.) but at other times it is used with an object such as the confession that Jesus [is] Christ (5:42), peace through Jesus Christ (10:36), the word (8:4) or the word of the Lord (15:35).

[5]This is what upset the Jewish authorities. See Acts 4:1-2; 5:28.

[6]Acts 9:22, 29; 18:4, 19, 28; 19:8-9. Significantly this sort of reasoning predominates in synagogues or where there is a starting point in Scripture. What seemed like madness to Festus, Paul defended as true and reasonable, something Agrippa, with some familiarity with Jewish things, could grasp (26:24-26).

[7]Acts 17:28, Titus 1:12. Perhaps 2 Timothy 4:13 also gives oblique testimony to this life-long commitment to reading.

functioning as an example to Timothy and other emerging leaders (1 Cor. 11:1; 2 Tim. 3:10 ff.). He instructed Timothy:

> Until I come, devote yourself to the public reading of Scripture, to preaching and teaching. Do not neglect your gift, which was given through a prophetic message when the body of elders laid their hands on you. Be diligent in these matters; give yourself wholly to them, so that everyone may see your progress (1 Tim. 4:13-15).

The charge not to neglect the use of his gift in the ministry of the word, but rather to devote himself to it, to be diligent in it, to give himself wholly to it, so all could see his progress, is surely an apostolic insistence upon *preparation* for preaching. Moreover, preaching itself prepares us to preach. Every time you use your gift you hone your ability to use it, learning from mistakes and being encouraged by triumphs of the word.

Preparation then involves the life-long disciplines of mind (meaning the whole of the inner life, including what we sometimes call the 'heart') and body in submission to God's word coupled with focused study that readies the preacher to expound a portion of that word. You will want to attend to both the long-term and immediate preparation. Horton Davies describes a time when Puritan John Howe's long-term preparation stood him in good stead:

> It appears that Cromwell wished to test John Howe as a chaplain. Summoning him to his camp headquarters, he gave him a text to study on the eve of the Sabbath. The next day, immediately after the prayer preceding the sermon, Cromwell altered the text which he had commanded Howe to expound; the worthy divine preached on the changed text until the monitory sands of the first and second hour had run out. Only when he was turning the hourglass for the third hour was he called upon to desist.[8]

---

[8]Horton Davies, *Worship and Theology in England: II. From Andrewes to Baxter and Fox, 1534–1690* (Grand Rapids: Eerdmans, 1996), 140.

# Part Two

# Preparing *Yourself* to Preach

# 4

# The Necessity and Centrality of Prayer

So far we have established that God is deeply committed to proclamation but that this does not mean we are without responsibility in preparing to preach. There are things we must do. We do our part by faith. The gracious initiative, power, and fruit-bearing potential all lie with God. Paul understood this.

> I became a servant of this gospel by the gift of God's grace given to me through the working of his power. Although I am less than the least of all God's people, this grace was given to me: to preach to the Gentiles the unsearchable riches of Christ, and to make plain to everyone the administration of this mystery (Eph. 3:7-9b).

Hear Paul again: 'But by the grace of God I am what I am and his grace to me was not without effect. No, I worked harder than all of them – yet not I, but the grace of God that was with me.' Paul links this hard work directly with proclamation in Colossians 1:28-29:

> We proclaim him, admonishing and teaching everyone with all wisdom so that we may present everyone perfect in Christ. To this end I labor, struggling with all his energy which so powerfully works in me.

The challenge for us as preachers is to take seriously our responsibilities, to work hard but to do so in such a way that we are not tempted to trust our efforts or even our gifts. When we rely on ourselves, preaching degenerates into mere oratory and rises no higher than humanly effective communication. Preaching, according to the Bible, is meant to be more – much more.

The reason we prepare *ourselves* to preach goes deeper than our responsibility to *do* certain things. Listen again to the apostle Paul as he continues in the same context:

> Now I rejoice in what was suffered for you, and I fill up in my flesh what is still lacking in regard to Christ's afflictions, for the

sake of his body, which is the church. I have become its servant by the commission God gave me *to present to you the word of God in its fullness* – the mystery that has been kept hidden for ages and generations, but is now disclosed to the saints. To them God has chosen to make known among the Gentiles the glorious riches of this mystery, which is *Christ in you* the hope of glory (Col. 1:24-27, italics added for emphasis).

The presentation of the word of God *in its fullness* is greatly enhanced by its truth being displayed in those who present it. The message, the mystery we are charged to present and long to see embodied in our listeners, is not just 'Christ' but 'Christ *in you* the hope of glory'. True, we proclaim *him*, that is Christ,[1] but in Colossians 2:1 Paul goes on to describe his struggles for those who had not met him. He wanted them to get the whole message, the word of God in its fullness. That meant setting before their eyes a picture of himself agonizing for the church. Only to hear his message and not see it would be like watching a television with sound but no picture. We can get the idea, but the picture, by definition, makes it vivid. You and I cannot separate what we say from who we are. We do not preach ourselves (2 Cor. 4:5), but we must prepare ourselves to preach, because proclamation is inevitably visual as well as verbal. Who we are will come through whether we want it to or not. Our lives either taint the gospel or adorn it.

Preparing yourself to preach requires disciplined attentiveness to several matters, matters of both being and doing. Before we consider them individually, we must dwell on the practice of prayer as it relates to preaching. Prayer is integral to preaching and is inextricable from every part of preparing to preach. Each chapter that follows could be prefaced by a paragraph on prayer – and several will be. But because preaching is something God wants to do through us, we must begin with a more foundational reminder of how prayer is at the heart of preaching.

---

[1]Colossians 1:28a, 2:2. Paul explicitly says in 2 Corinthians 4:5 that 'we do not preach ourselves but Jesus Christ as Lord, and ourselves as your servants for Jesus' sake'.

The logic of the centrality of prayer in preaching is this: If preaching is God speaking when we speak in his name, on his behalf, by his authority, and for the good of people to whom he has sent us, then we must speak his message. Of course that will mean that the message will be biblical, but the Bible is a large book and is easily misinterpreted. How do we know from all the possible thoughts available in the Bible, what he wants to say to the people he knows will be gathered to hear his word? We ask him. We wait quietly in his presence inviting him to speak to us as preachers through his word so that we can faithfully convey his message to our hearers. May our testimony be that of the Servant of the Lord:

> The Sovereign Lord has given me an instructed tongue, to know the word that sustains the weary. He wakens me morning by morning, wakens my ear to listen like one being taught. The Sovereign Lord has opened my ears, and I have not been rebellious; I have not drawn back (Isa. 50:4-5).

In that learning posture we ask that he speak in such a way that we will feed on the word and be reshaped by it. Then we will be able to thank God, as Paul said of the chosen among the Thessalonians, 'because our gospel came to you not simply with words, but also with power, with the Holy Spirit and with deep conviction. You know how we lived among you for your sake' (1 Thess. 1:5).

Jeremiah was God's messenger to Judah during the four decades just before the nation was taken into exile in Babylon. It was a tough assignment by any standard. What made it particularly challenging was that Jeremiah had to share the title 'prophet' with many who did not speak for God despite the fact that they claimed to do so. In Jeremiah 23 the Lord himself rails against these bogus representatives for lying in his name, for getting their messages from their own minds and dreams, and even for stealing material from one another rather than waiting upon him. Listen for the alternative the Lord wishes they had taken:

> But which of them has stood in the council of the Lord to see or to hear his word? Who has listened and heard his word? See, the

storm of the LORD will burst out in wrath, a whirlwind swirling
down on the heads of the wicked. The anger of the LORD will not
turn back until he fully accomplishes the purposes of his heart. In
days to come you will understand it clearly. I did not send these
prophets yet they have run with their message; I did not speak to
them, yet they have prophesied. *But if they had stood in my*
*council, they would have proclaimed my words to my people*
*and would have turned them from their evil ways and from*
*their evil deeds* (Jer. 23:18-22).

There is no substitute for standing in the council of God, entering his
presence with open Bibles and submissive minds. What a promise!
God promises to achieve repentance in our listeners when we wait
on him for his word to proclaim. We who have the whole canon of
Scripture need not wait for a *new* word from him, but must wait for
the Holy Spirit to illuminate what he has already written there. The
theater-goer can only see what is happening on the stage when two
conditions are met: The curtain must be drawn back and the lights
must be turned on. In revelation, God *unveils* the drama of
redemption. By his Spirit, he *illuminates* it so we can see it. In
prayer, we receive both of these gracious gifts, submitting our minds
to Scripture and inviting God himself to show us what he is saying
through it. We also ask that God would do the same for those who
hear us speak on his behalf.

One of the strange things about prayer is that too many of us, including
me, find it exceedingly difficult to practice it consistently and meaningfully.
Perhaps the reason is that prayer, as O. Hallesby helpfully reminds us, is
an act of helplessness.[2] We fail to pray when we think we don't need to
pray. Paradoxically, gaining more training as a preacher may have
precisely this unintended negative consequence. We learn more about
preaching, or gain some experience, and forget just how dependent we
are. To counter that danger we need constantly to remind ourselves of
reality. As Jesus put it, 'Apart from me you can do nothing' (John 15:5).
When we who preach pray about our preaching we are just facing
facts. To put it another way, prayer is an act of faith. When we proceed
to preach without prayer we are denying God's rightful place in the

---

[2]O. Hallesby, *Prayer* (London: InterVarsity, 1948), 13-21.

process and exalting our place far beyond God's calling. When we pray we are tangibly and specifically confessing our faith in what God has done, is doing, and will do. We are putting knees to what we profess.

What do we pray? We ask God to lead us to the right biblical books to expound and the right themes to be underscored. We pray for freedom from individual or cultural biases and eyes to see what the passage really teaches. We ask the Holy Spirit to be our teacher. We pray for faith to believe that God can speak to us and through us and that our responses to his word will be squarely in keeping with his revealed will. We pray for insights and clarity when we are stuck, for eyes to see faults in our expositions, for patience as we labor, and for love for our listeners and joy in serving them. We are asking for the Holy Spirit's illumination. There will be other requests as we progress in our preparation, but I recommend that you ask God often as you wait before him with Bible open, 'Lord, what do you want me to say from *this* passage to the people you know will be present this Lord's Day?'

Further, effective preaching is in a sense a cooperative effort. It involves the prayers of others in the body of Christ. If you restrict prayer for preaching to what *you* pray for your *own* preaching, you will have underestimated the depths of your need for God's work in you and for you. The apostle Paul made no such mistake. He asked those believers in the vicinity of Ephesus to pray that words would be given him whenever he opened his mouth and that he would preach fearlessly (Eph. 6:19-20). He asked the Colossians and Laodiceans to devote themselves to prayer for him and his fellow workers that the Lord would open a door for the word, that they would speak with the necessary clarity, and that the word would always be seasoned with grace (Col. 4:2-6). He asked the Thessalonians to pray that the word of the Lord would speed on its way and be glorified, just as it quickly found its way into their hearts (2 Thess. 3:1; see also 1 Thess. 1:2-10; 2:13-14). When we ask others to pray for us we invite them to join us in our struggle to serve God acceptably (Rom. 15:30-32). Many will be willing and grateful to do so.

Paul was mature enough not to make himself the sole focus of the prayers of the churches he served. He modeled sacrificial prayer for others. Among his ongoing requests for them was the following:

I keep asking that the God and Father of our Lord Jesus Christ, the glorious Father, may give you the Spirit of wisdom and revelation, so that you may know him better. I pray also that the eyes of your heart may be enlightened in order that you may know the hope to which he has called you, the riches of his glorious inheritance in the saints and his incomparably great power for us who believe (Eph. 1:17-19a).

If the word is to find good soil, our listeners must be prepared by prayer. Preaching, though not the only means, is one way God answers this prayer.

Paul asked that God's people would come to experience a richly Godward orientation, a renewed worldview with the Lord himself at his rightful place. This is instructive for us. Paul asked prayer for himself and his preaching, as we have seen. He was concerned about opportunity, words, clarity, and graciousness. More fundamentally, however, he wanted the word to renew the minds of his hearers so that they would see everything in a new light and live on the basis of that reality. Likewise, because prayer is an act of desperation, we may be tempted to restrict it to the things *we* feel desperate about. As Scripture transforms our own minds we will also pray about the ultimate things God cares about, things like the conformity of the church to his cosmic purpose.

Don't even think about preparing to preach without bathing the whole process in prayer. Recruit a number of life-long prayer warriors to stand with you in prayer. Make prayer the foundational discipline of every day. If you struggle with praying, make even that struggle a matter of fervent prayer.

God hears and answers prayer. Because preaching is speaking for and from God, we can't really preach until we have heard from God. That won't happen until we pray and God opens our ears to hear his word. We may rest assured, however, that when we and others truly seek God's help to hear and to preach his word for his glory, he will hear and answer. He has promised, 'I will do whatever you ask in my name, so that the Son may bring glory to the Father' (John 14:13).

# 5

## Preparing (or Repairing)
## Your Relationship with God

Unfortunately one does not have to read or listen long before hearing Christian teachers who leave the impression that if we merely follow certain 'biblical principles' we will be assured of success in life and ministry. If they mean that some biblical truths are more foundational than others, we would all agree. However, the teachers I have in mind often treat the principles they discover as laws of the universe that function on their own, without taking into account the activity of the living God. They set forth general laws of leadership or life that may be appropriated by anyone, and that purport to work for anyone, whether believer or unbeliever. These principles are presumed there for the taking, available to anyone smart enough to notice and employ them.

Contrary to such a notion, the Bible does not set forth impersonal laws of the universe that, like electricity, have to operate providing that one merely 'plug into' them. Rather, the principles articulated in the Bible show us how God usually works. They are never to be treated as rules for living or leading that neglect God himself. For instance, the Bible *does* affirm, 'A man reaps what he sows' (Gal. 6:7). But it places that principle of cause and effect squarely in the context of God's active involvement in the world he created and sustains. It is prefaced by the words, 'Do not be deceived: God cannot be mocked.' Thus, the saying about sowing and reaping was not given for people to do what is right in order merely to enjoy the *predictably* happy consequences of externally good behavior and avoid *predictably* painful consequences of externally wrong acts. That is why, for instance, when Peter admonishes his readers to humble themselves, he includes the biblical reminder, 'God opposes the proud but gives grace to the humble' (1 Pet. 5:5, quoting Prov. 3:34). God has not revealed ideas about his world to

37

be used for our benefit while he is neglected. He is the one to be reckoned with. Jesus would not have us take ideas *from God* with the faulty notion that we can use them without relating rightly *to God* himself. As he says in John 15:4-8:

> Remain in me, and I will remain in you. No branch can bear fruit by itself; it must remain in the vine. Neither can you bear fruit unless you remain in me. I am the vine; you are the branches. If a man remains in me and I in him, he will bear much fruit; apart from me you can do nothing. If anyone does not remain in me, he is like a branch that is thrown away and withers; such branches are picked up, thrown into the fire and burned. If you remain in me and my words remain in you, ask whatever you wish, and it will be given you. This is to my Father's glory, that you bear much fruit, showing yourselves to be my disciples.

Notice the negative and the positive of Christ's words. On our own, we cannot bear fruit. That is, we cannot manifest the maturity that expresses our reason for existence and makes us capable of reproduction. Failure to bear fruit is not just unfortunate; it is grounds for judgment. Positively, when we maintain a vital relationship with Jesus, we do bear fruit, much fruit, God-honoring fruit, fruit that demonstrates that we are truly disciples of Jesus. How? When the word of Jesus dwells in us, we ask rightly in prayer and God gives us what we ask because we ask for what honors the Lord.

The Lord Jesus himself modeled this vital relationship with the Father as an example of the relationship that we are also to have. Over one hundred times in John's Gospel the Savior describes his complete reliance upon the Father. For instance, he does so in terms of mutual indwelling in John 14:10-11a, when he says, 'Don't you believe that I am in the Father, and that the Father is in me? The words I say to you I do not speak from myself, but the Father who dwells in me does his works. Believe me that I am in the Father and the Father is in me.' If we want the Father to work when we speak in his name, we must dwell in him and let him live in us. We must attend to our relationship with God. Like any relationship this takes the time, effort, and openness that flow from genuine love. Like any relationship, neglect makes restoration increasingly difficult.

The danger for most preachers is not deliberate coldness toward God, but the almost imperceptible drift against which the writer to the Hebrews warns (Heb. 2:1). After prescribing careful attention, he describes our great salvation, focusing on Jesus its author. His exhortation follows: 'Fix your thoughts on Jesus, the apostle and high priest whom we confess' (Heb. 3:1). The best starting point to regain vitality and to stop the drift is to think about Jesus and glory in his matchless person and work. His love will rekindle our own (see 1 John 4:7-21 for a reminder of the dynamic involved). We will not be able to think long of Jesus without being grateful as well for both the ministries of the Holy Spirit who indwells us and the Father who purposed our salvation from eternity and chose us in Christ.

Perhaps you need more than a gentle reminder. Maybe you need a shock to jolt you wide awake to the dangers of drift and neglect. An Old Testament story has served that purpose for me. It concerns a great hero of the faith who spoke with God face to face yet made a serious mistake as God's spokesman precisely because of confusion in his relationship with God. The person is Moses, and the story is recorded in Numbers 20. The Israelite community was in the Desert of Zin. They had run out of water. The people opposed Moses and Aaron, quarreled and complained, wishing themselves dead – and laid the blame squarely at Moses' feet.

Moses and Aaron began by responding well. They sought the Lord at the entrance to the Tent of Meeting and he appeared to them. The Lord gave specific instructions: take the staff, gather the assembly, and *speak* to the rock before their eyes and it will pour out its water. God graciously promised, 'You will bring water out of the rock for the community so they and their livestock can drink' (Num. 20:8).

Moses followed the first two parts of the instruction precisely. He took the staff just as commanded. He and Aaron gathered the assembly. Then things went terribly wrong. Instead of *speaking* to the rock, Moses stood in front of the rock and said to the assembled community, 'Listen you rebels, must *we* bring you water out of this rock?' (Num. 20:10). He *said* the wrong thing. But matters got worse. He then *did* the wrong thing. 'Then Moses raised his arm and struck the rock twice with his staff. Water gushed out, and the community and their livestock drank' (Num. 20:11). Pause to notice that at one level Moses succeeded. The water gushed out and the community and their livestock drank. In the next verse however, we hear the Lord rebuke Moses and Aaron: 'Because you did not trust in me enough to honor me as holy in the sight of the Israelites, you will not bring this community into the land I give them.' It was a serious charge accompanied by a devastating consequence. Moses and Aaron had failed to treat the Lord as holy. Moses had said, 'Must *we* bring you water out of this rock?' He had confused himself with the living God, as if the rebels were all on one side of some imaginary line and he, Aaron and God were on the other. Moses had exalted himself, as if he, and not God, somehow had the power to bring forth water out of a rock. We do not portray God as holy when we confuse ourselves with him.

Perhaps by a few sanctified inferences we may see why he struck the rock instead of speaking to it. Exodus 17 records a similar experience that took place earlier. There the Lord commanded Moses to *strike* the rock and promised that he would stand there and that water would come out of the rock for the people. Moses obeyed and the water flowed. The leadership crisis was averted. Later, in the Numbers 20 account, the instructions were different. God told Moses to *speak* to the rock. Could it be that Moses was relying on a practice that 'worked' once before? Is it possible that a previous success now became in his mind a *principle of ministry*? ('Whenever God's people need water, strike the rock and water will flow.') If so, this is what the Lord calls failure to trust him, failure to treat him as holy.

This passage is a warning to the successful, to those who have heard God's voice in the past and now reckon they know what to do to get results. At the heart of Moses' failure was a faulty relationship with the Lord. Moses thought too highly of himself, despised the weakness of the community, and commandeered – or tried to commandeer – God's power. Instead of walking closely with the Lord and relying upon him, Moses and Aaron relied upon a past experience of God's power and so dishonored the Holy One. This was sin, and they paid dearly for it.

I invite you now to take some time to re-read Numbers 20 and ask the Lord to protect you from any such abuse of your relationship with him. Those who speak the word of God run the constant temptation of confusing themselves with God. May it never happen to you or to me.

# 6

## Relationships with Other
## People and Your Behavior

Next to your relationship with God, a close second in importance in preparing yourself to preach is to attend to your relationships with other people. This includes those who are not necessarily your listeners as well as those who are. Preaching, like other sacrificial ministries, means pouring out your life like a drink offering on the faith of others (Phil. 2:17). As such, Jesus' counsel in Matthew 5:23-4 applies to us who preach, 'Therefore, if you are offering your gift at the altar and there remember that your brother has something against you, leave your gift there in front of the altar. First go and be reconciled to your brother; then come and offer your gift.' If you have a broken relationship with someone, you may be preoccupied and unable to hear God's still, small voice. If you are estranged from one of your listeners, he or she will almost certainly discount what you say. God may well withhold his blessing. That is why Paul counsels men everywhere to lift up holy hands in prayer, *without anger or disputing* (1 Tim. 2:8, emphasis added).

An overseer must have good relationships in public and private. Fellow church members consider him above reproach. His wife and children know him to be faithful and a good leader. Outsiders see the same man of integrity as family and church members do (1 Tim. 3:1-7). Those who are single are not disqualified from teaching and preaching ministries and may find that singleness allows them to focus on the Lord's affairs, as apparently was the case with Paul (1 Cor. 7:27-31). They too are to set an example in every respect (see Titus 2:6-8 and 1 Tim. 4:12). If relationships are marred, a man may have an aptitude to teach but still be disqualified as an overseer.

The importance of good relationships with others is not merely negative. When Paul spoke of his team's ministry in Thessalonica he could appeal not only to God as his witness (1 Thess. 2:5), but also to the Thessalonians. They too knew the missionaries' pure motives, avoidance of flattery and greed, and disinterest in the praise of people. They could testify to their hard work and their unwillingness to be a burden. Paul, Silas, and Timothy loved the Thessalonians like both a mother and a father and were delighted to share with them not only the gospel but their very lives as well (1 Thess. 2:1-12). Their relationships were exemplary. Your listeners can tell if you love them, and they will know if you don't.

If your relationship with anyone is broken, strained, or even questionable, take the initiative to be reconciled. Assume that any fault is yours and be eager to confess it. This is why the discipline of coming regularly and often to the Lord's Table is so important. As part of diligent self-examination, ask the Lord to search you for broken relationships. Then confess your faults and be reconciled. Better still, work hard at relationships by investing the time and interest to listen, share your life, and serve.

Why is this so important for the preacher? The first and greatest commandment is to love the Lord with all you are and have; the second is to love your neighbor as yourself. During his last meal with the disciples before his crucifixion, Jesus explains how loving others, that is, how we relate to them, is at the core of the gospel:

> As the Father has loved me, so have I loved you. Now remain in my love. If you obey my commands, you will remain in my love, just as I have obeyed my Father's commands and remain in his love. I have told you this so that my joy may be in you and that your joy may be complete. My command is this: Love each other as I have loved you (John 15:9-12).

We remain in Christ by obeying him. We obey him by loving others as he loved us; as a result, his joy is in us and our joy is complete. Our relationship with Jesus – and therefore our ability to hear his voice – depends in no small measure on loving each other as he loved us.

## Your Behavior

Paul exhorted Timothy to devote himself to the public reading of Scripture, to preaching, and to teaching (1 Tim. 4:13). In the church where Timothy served, certain men devoted themselves to myths and endless genealogies. The results were controversies and meaningless talk (1 Tim. 1:3-7). Timothy was to counter this false teaching not only by proclaiming the truth but by living it. He was to be an example of sound doctrine 'in speech, in life, in love, in faith, and in purity'. Paul urged him, 'Watch your life and doctrine closely. Persevere in them, because if you do, you will save both yourself and your hearers' (1 Tim. 4:12, 16).

Later, in 2 Timothy 2:14-26, he reinforced this counsel by describing some consequences of *not* watching our lives and doctrine. They include more ungodliness, ruining our listeners, godless chatter, and false teaching that spreads like gangrene, sometimes destroying faith. The remedy is to cleanse oneself of all that is ignoble, flee youthful lusts, and pursue righteousness, faith and love in fellowship with others who call on the Lord out of a pure heart. Those who do this will be 'made holy, useful to the Master and *prepared* to do any good work'. This instruction is placed squarely in the context of the preacher's accountability to God. 'Do your best to present yourself *to God* as one approved, a workman who does not need to be ashamed and who correctly handles the word of truth' (2 Tim. 2:15). Our handling of God's word cannot be divorced from the lifestyle we live. We won't be ready for the good work of preaching unless we habitually, indeed, continually, cleanse ourselves, flee youthful lusts, and pursue godliness. Obedience affects both our being and our doing. As Peter writes, 'Having purified your souls by your obedience to the truth for a sincere brotherly love, love one another earnestly from a pure heart' (1 Pet. 1:22). Obedience to the truth purifies the soul, the very personality of the preacher, freeing us to love one another deeply. John implies that it goes well with the souls of those who walk in the truth (3 John 2-3).

By contrast, those who are 'loaded down with sins and swayed by all kinds of evil desires' are also described as 'always learning but never able to acknowledge the truth' (2 Tim. 3:7-8). Those who do not obey in faith sabotage their ability to understand the truth, to live the truth, or to benefit from it. We cannot preach what we do not know, do not live, and do not enjoy.

You and I are not ready even to prepare to preach until we have confessed our sins, turned from them, and turned toward God in an eager, sustained pursuit. We joyfully affirm that 'there is now no condemnation to those who are in Christ Jesus' (Rom. 8:1). At the same time, 'we know that anyone born of God does not continue to sin' (1 John 5:18). Consequently, we must work out our salvation with fear and trembling, knowing that it is God who works in us to will and to act according to his good purposes (Phil. 2:12-13). When he works in us and we work out what he is working in us, we become oaks of righteousness, a planting of the Lord for the display of his splendor (Isa. 61:3). Acorns from those oaks give birth to others like them.

# Part Three:

## Preparing Your Mind,
## Your Body, and the Congregation

# 7

## Preparing Your Mind (1)

Once you have assessed and addressed your relationships with God and others and repented of your sins, setting your course again to pursue God, you can give attention to your mind. We have what the apostle Paul calls 'the mind of Christ' and for that reason have the *capacity* to learn spiritual truth, the *content* that the Bible teaches. In other words, we can understand revelation in the way we could not without the Spirit. We can then use that revealed truth to test everything else (1 Cor. 2:6-16).

It is in the mind that the spiritual battle rages. Satan is a liar and deceiver as well as an accuser. Having lost ownership of us who believe, he can no longer command our obedience so he craftily seeks to twist our thinking to gain our compliance by stealth. His counterfeits, when embraced, undermine all that God intends when we preach. Our challenge is to keep in mind what God wants to achieve by our preaching. That means thinking God's thoughts about God himself, about the Bible, about preaching, about ourselves as preachers, about our listeners, about the church, about the world, about the devil, and about history. In short, we need a theology of preaching – a growing, working understanding of why God chooses to speak through people like you and me and how we can cooperate with him in that process.

I say *growing* because, as a preacher who is constantly studying the Bible, you will often see examples and precepts that enrich your understanding of how God wants to speak through you. These will refresh your understanding of your call, will correct misunderstandings, and will rebuke bad habits and neglectfulness. Other books, wisely chosen and diligently read, will also help. Your own practice of preaching will stir up a hunger to be more faithful, clearer in expression, and more sensitive to your listeners. These appetites, when expressed in the context of a hunger and thirst for God himself, will keep you growing as a preacher.

A good starting place for preparing one's mind to preach is a humble recognition of the greatness of your need. Although we may wish it were not so, we tend to see in Scripture only those things we know to look for. Therefore, the more we know of Scripture and its teachings, the more we will see in its pages. What we see today in the Bible will confirm, correct, extend, and illustrate what we saw earlier. Our study tomorrow will build upon what we learned today. The preacher who thinks he has seen all there is to see on a subject forfeits insights that might be his. Bible study then only reinforces what he already believes. But when we are hungry to devour every morsel of Scripture and invite the Spirit to fill our minds with the truths of each passage we study, the insights gained are like a magnifying glass that helps us see related truths in other passages. Listening to good preaching and reading good books will help us see truths we missed. Those truths will be part of our tool kit for mining more truth from God's word.

In that light, consider what follows to be a skeleton or outline of how biblical truths can shape your practice of preaching. What we could say about each of these subjects is almost limitless. The sound, biblical thoughts they trigger in your mind may be more helpful than the ones contained here. Let your mind be renewed as you think about God's work through you and in your listeners as you preach. Let the truths of Scripture become the objects of your contemplations and meditations. Ruminate, asking the Holy Spirit to put the right truths into the right patterns. Those thoughts will shape how you prepare to preach. Consider this a sampler of the kind of thinking you will want to do as you prepare to preach.

### Thinking rightly about God

Right understanding leads to right reading. This is mercifully given to those who preach by the Spirit of God (2 Cor. 4:1-4). If we expect to see in Scripture something other than what God wants us to see, we will miss what he has for us. God's purpose in Scripture is the display of his glory. Ours when we speak is to set forth the glory of God in the face of Christ (2 Cor. 4:6). The more we know about God from our study of Scripture, the more we will see and declare of him in each text we expound.

God is triune. All three persons of the Godhead are active in making the glory of the Father known to the nations and beyond, through God's people who display his multifaceted wisdom (Eph. 3:10). As preachers we must keep in mind those things about the Father that help us rely on him, and preach in ways that honor him. For instance, the Father is actively working out his purposes in us and in others.[1] He speaks,[2] and when he does so he does not lie.[3] Consequently, when we speak on his behalf we can expect him to speak through us and must be careful only to speak what is true.[4] It is through his word that he gives new life, so we can expect people to be born anew when we speak his word in his name.[5] Because God makes the wisdom of the world foolish we don't rely upon it or our own eloquence when we preach; instead, we affirm in what we say and how we say it that God's message delivered for his honor is truly powerful (1 Cor. 1:26–2:6). Knowing that we have the ministry of preaching because of God's mercy, we renounce any technique unworthy of him – secret, shameful ways, deceit, and distortion. Instead, we set forth the truth plainly, preaching in the sight of God and appealing to the consciences of our listeners. When people reject the message it is because Satan has blinded them. We don't make ourselves the subject of our preaching; we are only servants of the word we relay and servants of the God of the word (2 Cor. 4:1-7).

Because God is infinite, we need not worry about a shortage of material for our sermons. Because he is eternal, we need not fret that our message will lose its currency. Because God is gracious, our messages ought always to be gracious. Every sermon can be

---

[1] Philippians 2:13; Acts 14:27; 15:4, 12; 19:11; 21:19; Hebrews 13:20-21.

[2] Hebrews 1:1-2; 1 Thessalonians 2:13.

[3] Psalms 33:4; 119:160; Titus 1:2.

[4] 2 Corinthians 5:20; 1 Peter 4:11; 1 Timothy 2:7. Notice how the apostle Paul calls upon the triune God to testify of his truthfulness in Romans 9:1 and 2 Corinthians 11:31.

[5] 1 Peter 1:23; James 1:18; 1 Corinthians 4:6; Acts 10:34-48.

good news even when it contains a rebuke or exposes sin. Because God is holy, our listeners should never leave worship thinking that God is just like us. Because God is infinitely mighty, we need not use gimmicks to instill our sermons with power, but can speak with quiet but forceful confidence. We who are called to raise our voices with a message from him can do so without fear. Are you afraid that you will fail, that your life will be a waste, that your message will be rejected, that you will be written off? These real fears need not paralyze us because God is God and we speak in his name.

The Lord Jesus is God the Son. He too is alive and eternal, always living to make intercession for us. He humbled himself, took on our flesh, lived our life, died in our place, was raised immortal, ascended into heaven, and one day will come in power and great glory to save, judge, and reign. He himself is our message. His cross created the gospel we proclaim and the church we serve.[6] It is this gospel that gives us as preachers our identity (Eph. 3:7; 2 Tim. 1:8-12). Christ himself is at the center of the good news, and we preach him as such; like the Father, we want Jesus to have the supremacy in all things (Col. 1:18). Because Jesus is our Savior who now indwells us, we are walking visual aids of his power. On his behalf we appeal to people to be reconciled to God (2 Cor. 5:20). Indeed, he speaks through us (2 Cor. 13:3). We instruct with his authority.[7] Not only do we preach Christ (2 Cor. 4:5), we speak *in Christ* (2 Cor. 2:17; 12:19). We preach in the sight of God as those who enjoy everything that is ours by virtue of our union with Christ. Indeed, we indentify with Christ especially in his death and resurrection, his cross-bearing and his victory. The Lord Jesus is our creator and sustainer. All the strength we need is supplied by none other than the Lord of the universe and Lord over everything *for the church* (Eph. 1:18-23). Jesus understands our weaknesses and temptations. Through him we have access to the Father. He is our advocate and high priest through whom we offer our sermons

---

[6] 1 Corinthians 1:23; 2:2; 1 Thessalonians 2:4; Colossians 1:3-7; 2 Thessalonians 2:13-15.

[7] 1 Thessalonains 4:2. Though this verse refers to the apostle Paul and his team, Titus 2:15 implies that the authority is not limited to the apostles.

to God and upon whom we rely to make them acceptable sacrifices. Through him alone God is truly glorified.[8] Because our Lord Jesus will judge the secret things of every heart, every idle word, and every work, we seek to walk in the light and urge others to join us in appropriating his abundant grace.[9] Because he is our hope we labor in anticipation of future grace.[10] Because he promises to build his church, we can work hard in its service (Matt. 16:18; 1 Tim. 5:17).

In addition to these lofty things, he is also our example as preachers. Although equal with God, Jesus could say, 'For I have not spoken on my own authority, but the Father who sent me has himself given me a commandment – what to say and what to speak. And I know that his commandment is eternal life. What I say, therefore, I say as the Father has told me' (John 12:49-50, ESV). In his high priestly prayer, the Lord Jesus affirmed of his disciples, 'Now they know that everything you have given me comes from you. For I gave them the words you gave me and they accepted them' (John 17:7-8a). Jesus relied on the Father for the very words to speak.

The Holy Spirit is the Spirit of God and the Spirit of Jesus. He is quietly at work bringing glory to the Father through the Son (John 16:14; 14:13). As preachers, we are indebted to his finished work of inspiring the Scriptures, and his continuing work of illuminating them for us in the study and pulpit and for our listeners in the assembly. He gives gifts of wisdom, knowledge and teaching to the pastors and teachers he gives the church (Eph. 4:11-12; 1 Tim. 3:2). Because he regenerates both preacher and hearers, we who speak for God speak to equals, our brothers and sisters. He intercedes for us, helping us in our weakness (Rom. 8:26-27). He enables our speaking.[11] When God makes us competent as ministers of the new covenant, he does it by the Holy Spirit who gives life to the words we preach (2 Cor. 3:1-6).

---

[8] 1 John 2:1; Colossians 3:17; Philippians 2:16-18; Romans 15:15-18; 16:27; 2 Corinthians 1:20; Hebrews 13:15.

[9] Matthew 12:36; Romans 2:16; Acts 10:42.

[10] Romans 5:1-5; 2 Corinthians 3:12; 2 Thessalonians 2:16-17.

[11] Acts 1:2, 8, 16; 4:25; 11:28; 1 Thessalonians 1:5.

These thoughts only begin to recount all we have in God for which we can be grateful as preachers. Our posture as we prepare to preach is one of humble gratitude, rejoicing in all that God's presence with us brings. He truly is our sufficiency.

## Thinking rightly about the Bible

Among Paul's last recorded words to Timothy is this solemn charge: 'Preach the word' (2 Tim. 4:2). The context reveals an unbreakable link between the source and nature of Scripture and the task of preaching. The *source* of Scripture dictates its nature. The nature of Scripture suits it to its purpose. Its purpose will be achieved when we let it dictate what and how we preach.

The apostle Paul wanted his protégé Timothy to preach the right message in the right way for the right reasons. So in 2 Timothy 3:1-4:5, he contrasts his own life and teaching with the depraved opponents of the truth Timothy will encounter, challenging Timothy to follow apostolic doctrine because he knows both from whom he heard it and its saving power. Then he describes the Bible's source and usefulness and charges him to preach it in ways that fit both:

> All Scripture is God-breathed and is useful for teaching, rebuking, correcting and training in righteousness, so that the man of God may be thoroughly equipped for every good work. In the presence of God and of Christ Jesus, who will judge the living and the dead, and in view of his appearing and his kingdom, I give you this charge: Preach the Word; be prepared in season and out of season; correct, rebuke and encourage – with great patience and careful instruction (2 Tim. 3:16–4:2).

Notice first the *source* of Scripture. 'All Scripture is *God*-breathed.' His Spirit moved the prophets and apostles to write it, enabling them to put in their own words precisely what he wanted them to say. He did this in ways that make it truly the word of God.

Consider next the *nature* of God's word. God's nature shapes its nature. For example, he lives; it lives (Heb. 4:12). He speaks; it speaks.[12]

---

[12]Isaiah 44:6 is one instance of many where God, unlike idols, speaks. B.B. Warfield documents the connection between the Bible and God's word in an

Because God speaks to be heard and obeyed, Scripture is clear enough to be obeyed.[13] Because God cannot lie, his word is true (Titus 1:2). Because God is almighty, his word is powerful (Isa. 44:24-28). He is eternal and so is his word (Isa. 40:28; 1 Pet. 1:25). He is all-knowing; his word is searching (Ps. 139; Heb. 4:12-13). Because God is holy, the Scriptures are holy (Rom. 1:2-4; 2 Tim. 3:15; Rev. 3:7). Paul's point in 2 Timothy 3:16-17 is that all Scripture, because it is all God-breathed, is useful. We turn now to consider those uses.

'All Scripture is ... *useful* for teaching, rebuking, correcting and training in righteousness, so that the man[14] of God may be thoroughly equipped for every good work.' The usefulness of Scripture is put in both immediate and more ultimate terms. The four immediate uses of the Bible (teaching, rebuking, correcting, and training in righteousness) achieve the larger purpose of equipping God's people so that they will be ready for every good work. Significantly, Paul's charge to preach the word is fleshed out by specific injunctions that largely correspond to the immediate uses of Scripture. The Bible is profitable for teaching; preachers are to engage in patient and careful instruction. The Bible is useful for rebuking and correcting; preachers of the word are to rebuke and correct. The nature of the Bible shapes, even dictates, the nature of preaching. The Bible itself reveals God, his ways, and his plan. It teaches truth. It is the Spirit's agent in regeneration (Jas. 1:18; 1 Pet. 1:23). It exposes sin in all its forms. It goes to work in us sanctifying us (1 Thess. 2:13; John 17:17). It does these things to equip us to serve so that the church may be built up and God glorified. Our sermons should strive to achieve the purposes for which Scripture was given.

How then does a growing, increasingly accurate view of the Bible shape our preaching? First, it *removes some major temptations* in

---

essay entitled, "'It Says:' 'Scripture Says:' 'God Says,'" *The Inspiration and Authority of Scripture* (Philadelphia: Presbyterian and Reformed, 1970), 299-348.

[13] 2 Corinthians 1:13; 4:2. This does not mean that every part of the Bible is easy to understand or incapable of being distorted. See 2 Peter 3:16.

[14] The word here is *anthrōpos* and refers to men and women. Scripture is designed by God to equip all of us.

preaching. In Paul's defense of his ministry to the Corinthians he argues that he renounced secret and shameful ways, including deception and distortion of the word of God (2 Cor. 4:2). He was able to resist these temptations precisely because he was preaching the word of God. He could not preach a word that is true and do so deceitfully. He did not need to engage in manipulation because the gospel doesn't need that. It is powerful enough to save without the help of devious strategies. If the gospel were veiled, the reason lay not in the plainly-preached message but in the blindness of the minds of unbelieving hearers who were perishing. He dared not distort the message for he knew he preached in the sight of God.

Second, right thinking about Scripture *restricts the content* of our sermons. Sermons are not to take as their subject whatever people are talking about or whatever their itching ears want to hear (2 Tim. 4:3). Faithful Christian preaching addresses those subjects the Bible addresses. The Bible is about the rightful reign of God – how it was rejected from the beginning and God's plan to restore it with Jesus Christ at its center as King of Kings and Lord of Lords. Jesus explained to the eleven how every part of Scripture points to him (Luke 24:27). We preach it all, confident that, in ways we can readily discern, it leads us to him. Sometimes it instructs (Rom. 4:23). Sometimes it provides examples that warn (1 Cor. 10:11). Always it speaks. We need not look beyond it for the subjects of our messages.

Third, preaching the Word *shapes our style*. The Bible is a rich tapestry of literary genres. In its pages we find stories, history, law, oracles, gospels, letters, and apocalyptic writings. Some parts are written in poetry, some in prose. So, for instance, if I am preparing to expound Psalm 34, I will do the careful analytical study that we will explore in Part Four, but I will remember that poetry moves those who hear it by sounds and images and repetition, not just by ideas or concepts. Consequently, I will help my listeners envision the angel of the Lord encamping around those who fear him, the eyes of the Lord upon the righteous, and his ears listening for their cry. I will help them picture the surprising image of a weak, hungry lion – unlikely but possible – and contrast that with those who seek the Lord and lack no good thing.

When I expound one of Paul's epistles, I will remember the story behind the letter. Paul sometimes wrote from prison. Often he agonized over the new churches and baby Christians. The recipients faced specific challenges. When I preach I let the humanity of the letter shine through, although never at the expense of the truth the text is teaching. Some parts of the Bible build and sustain suspense; others get right to the point. I don't want to take something that is only there to set the stage and make that central to my sermon. For instance, if I am preaching from Esther or Jonah, I will remember that in each case the whole story conveys the main message of the book. If I make too much of Haman or the sailors, I risk missing the point of the story, perhaps because I have forgotten that it is a story. The entire Bible, no matter how lofty its subject matter, is written for real readers (or listeners, as is the case in many oral cultures). Our preaching gets a head start when we let the genre of the text influence how we shape our sermons. The variety, directness, and clarity of the Bible should come through in our messages. When the apostle Paul wanted to explain why we are free to live righteous lives, he used the analogy of slavery, explaining, 'I put this in human terms' (Rom. 6:19). We would do well to learn from him.

Fourth, understanding the purposes for which Scripture was given *clarifies our aim* in preaching. John limited what he included in his gospel with a *purpose:* 'that you may believe that Jesus is the Christ, the Son of God, and that by believing you may have life in his name' (John 20:31). His purpose is our most basic one. Building on the success of the word in making people wise unto salvation, we use that same word to thoroughly equip them for every good work. Although *teaching* is foundational, it is not enough. Doctrine provides the basis for addressing life, for *rebuking* and *correcting* and *equipping* people for service. If our preaching merely informs our listeners, or only challenges them academically or intellectually, we have not preached the Bible the way the Bible should be preached. By the same token, if we merely challenge people ethically or relationally, without using Scripture to conform their view of reality to God's view, we have failed to preach the Bible according to its own dictates. Preaching the Bible to conform minds, hearts, beliefs, and lives to the image of Christ takes patience and care (2 Tim. 4:2). That leads to a final way in which an accurate view of the Bible shapes our preaching.

Fifth, preaching the Bible according to its own nature *gives us hope*. Paul testified that in his ministry of plainly setting forth the truth he did not lose heart (2 Cor. 4:1-6). Why not? He knew from personal experience that some would receive the message for what it is, the word of God (1 Thess. 2:13). He knew first-hand the power of the word to establish and encourage believers (Acts 14:21-22; Rom. 16:25-27). In fact, he knew that the word has a life of its own. He and others taught and preached the word of the Lord (Acts 15:35-36). Sometimes, whole cities gathered to hear the word of the Lord. They were glad, honored the word of the Lord, and it spread through the whole region (Acts 13:44, 48, 49). The apostles' role was only to speak the word of the Lord boldly and plainly, in reliance upon the Holy Spirit and for the glory of God. Behind God's word stands God's promise, 'As the rain and the snow come down from heaven and do not return to it without watering the earth and making it bud and flourish, so that it yields seed for the sower and bread for the eater, so is my word that goes out of my mouth: It will not return to me empty but will accomplish what I desire and achieve the purpose for which I sent it' (Isa. 55:11). We rest in the hope that God's word always accomplishes his purposes, even when our preaching falls short of producing the immediate results we sought.

How then do we keep fresh in our minds the nature, purposes, and power of the word we proclaim? We do so first by saturating our minds and hearts with its words. We listen to it. We read it. We study it. We memorize it. We may even transcribe it as the kings of Israel were instructed to do (Deut. 18:20), using our own eyes and hands to make our own copy. We meditate on it, turning its truths over in our minds day and night. We read it in the original languages whenever possible. We listen to good sermons that expound it. We study books *about the Bible* when they are available to us. If God has given others the ability to understand Scripture and the specialized training to study it carefully, we are arrogant if we dismiss their insights without understanding, weighing, and considering them.

Next, and most importantly, we *obey* God's word. We heed it. Our submissive obedience to the truth we have received enables us to receive more truth (John 7:17; Col. 1:9-10). When we obey it, our own experience lends subjective confirmation of its objective truth. Finally, we teach it. Teaching what we have learned to someone else is the normal expectation of all growing Christians and is the requirement of those called to oversee the church (Heb. 5:12; 1 Tim. 3:2). Only when we can teach the Bible do we really grasp it. You may recognize this three-fold strategy as that of the faithful scribe, Ezra. 'For Ezra had set his heart to *study* the Law of the LORD, and to *do* it and to *teach* his statutes and rules in Israel' (Ezra 7:10 ESV, emphasis added).

# 8

## Preparing Your Mind (2)

### Thinking rightly about the task of preaching

I hope what you have read so far has given you a lofty view of preaching. It is a glorious task and high calling. It is a significant responsibility to be undertaken by those God has called to it. But to make sure we don't place it above where God places it, let us focus our thinking about preaching by recalling what it is not.

*Preaching is not the only ministry of the word.* Peter Adam helpfully reminds us that other ministries of the word include such things as evangelizing, training, counseling, public reading of Scripture, and writing.[1] By implication, Bible reading plans, Scripture memory, conversation, Sunday school, small groups, a good church library, Bible schools, and seminaries can be means or settings where the word is ministered. It is important to remember this in order not to put all the weight of the word's ministry on to the public oral discourse we call preaching. Preaching is key, but it is not the only place in church where God's message is heard. For example, when we eat the bread and drink the cup at the Lord's Table we *proclaim* the Lord's death until he comes (1 Cor. 11:26).

A corollary to this observation is that *sound biblical preaching is not to be thought of as God's solution to every problem in the church.* It is tempting to do one thing God has commanded and has promised to bless and assume falsely that everything else will be sorted out. The resulting strategy focuses on the latest solution to all the church's problems – now small groups; now reforming the eldership; now spiritual warfare; now thinking Christianly about the world. Then we experience discouragement when those efforts

---

[1]Peter Adam, *Speaking God's Words: A Practical Theology of Expository Preaching*, 59 ff.

do not solve problems they do not address. God-honoring preaching is foundational and indispensable, but does not claim to be all God asks of us and should not be treated as a cure-all. Instead, it should be seen as one of God's many gifts to the church to be stewarded, developed, and employed along with other gifts, graces, and disciplines.

Third, *preaching is not just one kind of speaking.* Bryan Chapell selects ten Old Testament words and twenty-four from the New Testament to 'indicate the diverse tasks of God's spokesmen'.[2] Peter Adam puts thirty-three words into five categories: words of information, declaration, exhortation, persuasion, and conversation.[3] The *Greek-English Lexicon of the New Testament Based on Semantic Domains* lists fifty-six subdomains under the domain 'Communication'. Under the six of these most relevant to preaching ('Inform, Announce'; 'Assert, Declare'; 'Teach'; 'Speak Truth, Speak Falsehood'; 'Preach, Proclaim'; 'Witness, Testify'), the authors list eighty-four words that relate to what we are called to do, or in the case of false teaching, to avoid.[4]

If you survey these words you will discover that speaking to people for God covers a wonderfully rich range of discourse. It includes such things as detailed speech relayed with the emphasis on clarity, describing the indescribable, revealing what was previously secret, and spreading information extensively. Some of these words contain the message in them; some tell us how the message is to be delivered; some build in the expected response. Some even remind us that we open the mouth to speak! When we think about the task of preaching, we should not limit ourselves to a single shape, style, or occasion, but recognize that in all sorts of ways, each consistent with his character, God wants to get his message into the lives of people and through them into the lives of more people. Preaching, as we seek to practice it, is declaring in God's name and by his power, from Scripture, what he placed there to achieve his ends for his glory.

---

[2]Bryan Chapell, *Christ-Centered Preaching*, 89-91.

[3]Peter Adam, *Speaking God's Words*, 75-76.

[4]Johannes P. Louw and Eugene A. Nida, *Greek-English Lexicon of the New Testament*, Vol. 1, 388-419.

## Thinking rightly about yourself as preacher

With all we have learned about God's commitment to preaching, you could easily think too highly of yourself or feel crushed by the weight of responsibility, despite God's gracious provision. Conversely, by focusing on what God does in preaching, you might think of yourself as someone passive in the process. To overcome these faulty ideas, we will do well to think of ourselves in the following terms: we are important, but not personally indispensable. We are dependent, but not irresponsible.

Preachers are important in God's economy. The Lord Jesus made it plain that preachers, empowered by the Holy Spirit, would go from Jerusalem to all the nations (Luke 24:46-49). Paul asks an important string of questions: 'How, then, can they call on the one they have not believed in? And how can they believe in the one of whom they have not heard? And how can they hear without someone preaching to them? And how can they preach unless they are sent?' (Rom. 10:14-15). The correct answer in each case is that they cannot. As God has ordained things, someone has to preach. God is not limited to you, but if you are one of those he has called, you are important, right along with those who send you.

When Philip asked the Ethiopian official if he understood the text of Isaiah he was reading, he replied, 'How can I unless someone guides me?' (Acts 8:31 ESV). So Philip began right there with that passage and preached the good news of Jesus. Without Philip it would not have happened, at least not that day in that way.

When Paul explained to Timothy and Titus how to ensure sound doctrine in the churches they served, he emphasized that overseers needed to be apt to teach (1 Tim. 3:2) and had to hold firmly to sound doctrine as it had been taught so they could encourage others with it and refute those who contradicted it (Titus 1:9). Titus was to appoint such elders *in every town*, and the canonical letter *Titus* apparently was not the first time Paul directed Titus to make such appointments (Titus 1:5).

Every church needs the kind of elders who can handle the word rightly for the health of the church. If you have been appointed to this task, you are important, although if you fall short, God is able to raise up others to do this task. We who preach are important, but not personally indispensable.

Alongside that conviction is another: In God's economy, preachers are dependent, although not like victims who are *irresponsibly* dependent. We are dependent upon God for words (1 Pet. 4:11). We are dependent upon the Lord Jesus for continual intercession on our behalf (Heb. 7:25; Rom. 8:34). We are dependent upon the Holy Spirit for gifts of teaching, for illumination, for anointing, and for quickening our listeners. We are dependent upon the church where our gifts are affirmed and developed and where, or on behalf of whom, our preaching takes place. To put it in terms of the biblical images, a herald can't declare a message he does not have. A sower needs seed to plant. An ambassador has to represent a sovereign. A servant needs a master. A shepherd is no shepherd without sheep. A builder or workman needs a building site or a field to do his work. A father derives that role from having children.[5] All of these biblical roles call for responsible action and hard work. In each case all we need is supplied along with sufficient instruction. Preaching requires, to adapt a phrase from the apostle Paul, 'faith that leads to obedience' (Rom. 1:5; 16:26). It is grace that frees us to work hard (1 Cor. 15:10-11). We trust God, relying upon his direct and indirect provisions, seeing them not as reasons to do nothing but as supplies that enable us to take the journey preachers must take. We are dependent, but it is a liberating dependence.

Preachers seem unusually susceptible to the sin of pride that manifests itself as arrogance and a sort of self-reliance that, in turn, often leads to debilitating insecurity. These miserable states do not 'adorn the gospel' (Titus 2:10). We may give in to the sin of sloth and even excuse it by hyper-spiritual talk about what God can do despite us. We may suffer from the malady of unwarranted discouragement which looks too early for fruit from seeds just planted. As long as we are in the flesh we will not completely be rid of these sins and this malady. Nevertheless, we can make visible progress by affirming in practice that the importance of our calling

---

[5]These biblical images are helpfully developed in John Stott, *The Preacher's Portrait* (Grand Rapids: Eerdmans, 1961).

does not make us indispensable and that our dependence upon God empowers us instead of victimizing us.

## Thinking rightly about your listeners

The learned Charles Simeon was a Fellow of King's College, Cambridge in England and became Vicar of Holy Trinity Church in 1783 where he had a long and fruitful ministry. He was committed to helping his students learn to preach. Of the wise counsel he offered them, some of the best he put quaintly.

> Do not preach what *you* can tell, but what your people can receive. Suppose I have six narrow-mouthed glass bottles to fill. I have both a large pail brimful of water and a small tea-kettle, with a taper spout, also full of water. Which of the two shall I use in filling the narrow-mouthed bottles?[6]

The question is not, 'What is the best sermon I can preach?' But 'What is the best sermon my listeners can hear?'

Not all listeners are the same. This may seem obvious, but it is easy to forget as you focus on preparing a message. Preparing your mind to think rightly includes thinking rightly about the individuals you will address. Of course in some ways we are all alike. All of us have been made in the image of God and in each of us that image is distorted. 'All have sinned and fall short of the glory of God' (Rom. 3:23). 'All we like sheep have gone astray' (Isa. 53:6). That combination of dignity and depravity shapes every human being. Yet, there are significant differences. In the parable of the soils, Jesus describes four possible responses to the preaching of the word (Mark 4:1-20). Some do not understand the word, and Satan actively snatches it away. Others respond superficially and the word does not take root. Still others find the word choked out by daily cares, the deceitfulness of wealth, and the desire for other things. Only a fraction actually go on to maturity and reproduce, and these do so in varying degrees. Paul recorded an encouraging response among the Thessalonians, but they were evidently a minority in their

---

[6]Charles Smyth, *The Art of Preaching: A Practical Survey of Preaching in the Church of England 747–1939* (London: SPCK, 1940), 176.

town. Nearby the Bereans in the local synagogue received the word eagerly and checked it by the Scriptures (Acts 17:11-12). The writer to the Hebrews warned his readers that they were in danger of drifting (Heb. 2:1) and were slow to learn. For them he had to review basic teachings, although by that time they should have been doing the teaching (Heb. 5:11-14). Paul warned Timothy that there would be those who were always learning but never able to acknowledge the truth (2 Tim. 3:7). Such people were both deceived and deceivers ( 2 Tim. 3:13).

Although it is not usually helpful to put people into categories, it is worth remembering as we prepare to preach that some to whom we preach are spiritually dead, blind, and deaf. The light has not dawned. Their eyes have not been opened to their sin or to Christ's ability to save. This distinction dwarfs all the others. It does not follow that we don't preach to these people or that when we do that we don't expect them to respond. On the contrary, we do preach to them and do expect a response because the Holy Spirit uses the word of God to give life and light (1 Pet. 1:23; James 1:18; 2 Cor. 4:6). We know that the same word will harden others who will choose to retreat into darkness (John 3:19-21). When people do respond to God with faith, God gets the credit, for as John the Baptist put it, 'A man can receive only what is given him from heaven' (John 3: 27. See also 1 Cor. 4:7). When people do not respond, God holds them accountable because they rejected the light he gave them (Rom. 1:18-32).

When we preach to a congregation in church we may feel confident that most have spiritual life. We see and hear their professions of faith, their love for God and flight from evil, their zeal for the gospel, and conclude that they have been born from above. Even here, however, we may be surprised (Matt. 7:21-23). With regard to others in whose lives we do not see evidence of God's grace, we may think them not yet reborn. Again, we may be incorrect in our assessment because we cannot see their hearts. In no case are we wise to presume. In the case of the unconverted we will pray that God will open blind eyes as we speak his word. In the case of the converted we will labor to establish them in the word.

Proclamation of the gospel in its broadest sense can serve both functions (Rom. 16:25). If we are wise, we will be alert to both sorts of hearers in every congregation we address.

Beyond this fundamental distinction, we should speak to all our listeners as sensible people who, despite the impact of the fall, can – with the help of the Holy Spirit – weigh our words and hold fast to what is good (1 Cor. 10:15; 1 Thess. 5:21). They will sense our respect for them and be more likely to give the word a hearing. On the other hand, we should not assume too much about anyone. Even the brightest of the reborn are 'weak in [their] natural selves' (Rom. 6:19). We should use analogies, images, and word pictures, as the Bible itself does, to make its thoughts plain to them.

The situation in which we speak will certainly dictate which things we say first, what we may generally assume, and how to appeal to our listeners. For instance, when Peter was addressing the close friends and relatives of Cornelius assembled at his home, he evidently assumed that even these Gentiles knew some things about the gospel, reminding his listeners, 'you know' as he reviewed some facts he could build upon.[7] Further, we should recall that women and men may not think in precisely the same ways.[8] Younger people may lack the perspective that comes with experience; older people may be tempted to assume they know everything, and so don't actually listen. Others, regardless of age categories, will defy any generalizations. Some will be new believers who lack a basic theological framework or Christian world view; your preaching, together with their reading and conversation, must gradually help them overcome these deficiencies. Some will be the faithful people called to equip others; they are listening not just for themselves but for those whom they are discipling. Some will be at church or in the

---

[7] Acts 10:37. See also Acts 17:2-4 for an example of how Paul reasoned from the Scriptures in the synagogues, how he gave law-keepers the benefit of the doubt in Acts 22:3, 12, and how in Acts 25:25-26 he took into account what King Agrippa knew and spoke in ways that were both true and reasonable, despite being perceived by Festus as madness.

[8] A helpful book for thinking this through is Alice P. Mathews, *Preaching That Speaks to Women* (Grand Rapids: Baker Academic, 2003).

gathering you address because of family or other social pressure, or by force of habit. Some will be there for reasons almost entirely unrelated to your aims in the preaching situation. Some will be very alert intellectually; others will be more limited. Some will have trained and filled their minds; others, sadly, will have either neglected their minds or filled them with lies, or don't expect to use them in church.[9] Some will be able to focus on your words; others will be distracted and preoccupied by all sorts of things, real and perceived. Some will be sleepy; others well rested. Some will come expecting merely to be entertained (Isa. 30:9-11).

What is our strategy in preaching to such a range of people? First and foremost, we pray, recalling that this is a spiritual battle. We pray that the light of the word will overcome the darkness in each mind, including our own. We pray for discernment as we prepare, that the Holy Spirit would lead us to the right text and enable us to say those things from it that would faithfully speak to the people whom God knows will be in attendance. We pray against distractions, internal and external. We pray that the seed will fall on some good soil.

Second, we prepare to preach with focus, recalling every sort of person present. We think of the new believer, the backslider, the person distracted by the weeds Jesus mentioned, the mature mother listening for herself and for her children, the single person grappling with issues long forgotten by married people. We then address them, at least in representative fashion, as the text gives us warrant and as time allows. We speak in God's name to the spiritually dead trusting that God will raise some to life. We speak to the holy to establish and encourage them. This means that we will apply the teachings of the text in various ways, always in keeping with the dictates of the passage, but tailored to the actual and perceived needs of our hearers. Our message may not connect with everyone each time we speak, but over time no listener should have reason to think we are only speaking to others. If we set forth the beauties of Christ every time we preach, it will be relevant to every person listening.

[9] 1 Corinthians 14:14 seems to envision such a danger.

Third, we remember that no individual will receive and bear fruit from everything we say or every time we speak. Some of the seed we sow will fall on good soil and bear lasting fruit to God's glory. Our goal is to be his messengers, speaking in such a way that his voice is heard and his people respond with the faith that leads to obedience.

To achieve these ends we need to seek to actually know the people to whom we speak, not merely to know about them. As Charles Bridges put it in 1830,

A pulpit Ministration may command attention and respect; but except the preacher convert himself into a Pastor, descending from the pulpit to the cottage, and in Christian simplicity 'becoming all things to all men'; there will be nothing that fastens on the affections – no 'bands of love'. The people cannot love an unknown and untried friend and confidence without love is an anomaly. The unintelligent, more influenced by impulse than by judgment, will probably unite themselves with Teachers upon their own level, with whom they live as fathers, brothers, and friends, in all the reciprocity of daily fellowship. We must therefore constantly aim at nearer contact, and closer interest with them; winning their hearts, as the way to win their souls –living among them in the interchange of those kindly offices, which (as Bishop Gibson admirably observed) 'are the means of endearing Ministers to their people, and of opening a passage into their hearts for spiritual instruction of all sorts'.[10]

## Thinking rightly about the Church

Thinking rightly about your listeners individually is not the same as thinking rightly about the church. Here we recall some basic truths about the Body of Christ that will help keep our preaching on track. These are important for the pastor-teacher who is an overseer or teaching elder of a local fellowship, but also for all those who minister the word alongside the local church and on its behalf. Whether parachurch workers, missionaries, or Bible Study Fellowship teachers, all of us

---

[10]Charles Bridges, *The Christian Ministry with an Inquiry into the Causes of its Inefficiency* (Carlisle, Penn; Banner of Truth, 1967), 352.

who publicly minister the word need to remember how we are to relate to the church. What do we need to recall?

First, the word of God created the church and not vice versa. Individual congregations came into being when preachers preached the word and the Holy Spirit granted repentance and faith. Later on, the church *recognized* what was included in the Bible, but they did not *create* it. The Bible is not the church's property to be adjusted and used for its purposes. Rather, the church is the *steward* of the word, and individual preachers are entrusted with it for those to whom it is given (1 Cor. 4:1-3). That is why Paul considered himself to be a debtor to Greeks and Barbarians and was eager to preach to the Romans (Rom. 1:14-15). God had entrusted the word to him for them, and until he delivered it to them, he was indebted to them. He had in his possession something that was not his own but was theirs. Until he delivered it, he was in their debt. If we succumb to the temptation to think of the word of God merely as a resource for our use, we will inevitably abuse it, adapting it to our purposes instead of letting it set our agenda.

Second, the church affirms God's call on preachers and authorizes their ministries. As we have already noted, this is an integral part of God's preparation of preachers. We underscore here that the church should select as overseers, elders, or pastor-teachers only those who meet the biblical qualifications.[11] Its leaders will not hesitate to commend publicly those whose gifts and calling it affirms.[12] Preachers are not to pursue free-lance, unaccountable preaching ministries answerable to no one. The church has too often been severely injured by the 'ministries' of those who were not properly authorized and who are accountable to no one.

Third, the church exists for the glory of God, not to meet the needs of the pastor. 'His intent was that now, *through the church,*

---

[11] 1 Timothy 3:1-7; Titus 1: 5-9. In Acts 20:17, 28 Paul addresses elders whom he calls overseers, a role that calls upon them to shepherd the flock. In Titus 1:5-9 he directs Titus to appoint elders, whom he calls 'overseers' in verse 7. Different denominations select leaders in different ways.

[12] Notice, for instance, Acts 16:2; 18:27-28; 1 Corinthians 16:10, 15-18; Philippians 2:19-30; Colossians 4:7, 9.

the manifold wisdom of God should be made known' (Eph. 3:10, emphasis added). The Sovereign Lord pronounces a woe against those shepherds who only take care of themselves. They eat the curds, clothe themselves with the wool, even slaughter the choice animals, but do not take care of the flock (Ezek. 34:1-6). It is true that the flock is commanded in Scripture to support its shepherds tangibly and intangibly.[13] Furthermore, the shepherd has a responsibility to pay careful attention to himself (Acts 20:28). Nevertheless, he does this so that he may take care of the flock. We are to feed and protect the sheep, searching for the lost, strengthening the weak, healing the sick, binding up the injured, and looking for the strays. Like the Good Shepherd, we lay down our lives for the sheep instead of ruling them harshly or lording it over them (1 Pet. 5:3). A shepherd bears burdens instead of becoming a burden. As Paul noted, 'After all, children should not have to save up for their parents, but parents for their children. So I will very gladly spend for you everything I have and expend myself as well' (2 Cor. 12:14-15). An entitlement mentality in a preacher is an ugly thing and a hindrance to the gospel. We are entitled only to the cross.

Fourth, churches are responsible to instruct, and when necessary, discipline their pastors, including those who preach. The equipping of the saints is the calling of the four gifted office bearers: apostles, prophets, evangelists, and pastor-teachers (Eph. 4:11-12). When they use their gifts and graces to equip the whole body, some of those they equip will have gifts of teaching and will ultimately be called to the role of pastor-teacher. Individual churches may band together to supplement this equipping of equippers, but the seminaries or other training ministries they form only function as servants of the church and should do so under proper authority. Perhaps the best of this equipping will happen informally, as when Priscilla and Aquila mentored Apollos (Acts 18:24-28). The other side of instruction is the public rebuke, which teaches both the elder and the church. This sort of discipline is necessary because the church

---

[13]Galatians 6:6; 1 Corinthians 9:7-14; 1 Timothy 5:17-18; Hebrews 13:17; 1 Thessalonians 5:12-13.

cannot function as a pillar and foundation of the truth when its leaders stray from that truth either by what they teach or how they live (1 Tim. 3:15; 5:19-21). Parachurch workers who teach the Bible may need to seek out this sort of oversight.

Fifth, the church is shepherded primarily, though not exclusively, by the ministry of the word. The role of pastor-teacher implies that the two functions of shepherding and teaching are linked. Pastors see to it that the sheep are fed. The ministry of the word, including preaching, is a manifestation of pastoral care. In practice, it is tempting to think of pastoral care and preparing to preach as competing with one another. Both take time and time is limited. When we are not clear about how the two relate, we may neglect the one to give more emphasis to the other. In fact, preparing to preach is a good investment of pastoral time. Preparing a nourishing spiritual meal for the whole congregation multiplies the time invested by the pastor.

Sixth, the church, by its response to preaching, helps the preacher determine what to preach next and at what depth. When Jesus' followers heard his demanding teaching about eating his flesh and drinking his blood they complained, 'This is a hard teaching. Who can accept it?' The text immediately records how Jesus tailored his next remarks to address their initial response, '*Aware that his disciples were grumbling about this*, Jesus said to them ...'[14] The writer to the Hebrews judged his listeners to be 'slow to learn' and cut back his letter accordingly (Heb. 5:11; 13:22). Our teaching likewise needs to be *dialogical*. We listen and watch for the response of our listeners and then faithfully press home the message of Scripture in ways they are able to hear. This does not imply omitting or soft-pedaling profound truths, hard sayings, or demanding duties. It does mean speaking intelligibly for understanding. We do this because 'when anyone hears the message about the kingdom *and does not understand it*, the evil one comes and snatches away what was sown in his heart' (Matt. 13:19). Neither do we talk down

---

[14]John 6:60-61. See also 1 Thessalonians 1:13-14; 3:6-10; 4:1-2; and Galatians 1:6 for contrasting messages related largely to the responses of these congregations to earlier teaching.

to our listeners. We deal gently with the ignorant and wayward because we too are weak (Heb. 5:2). We are to be patient with everyone (1 Thess. 5:14; 2 Tim. 4:2). As discerning observers and listeners we, together with fellow elders, will assess strengths and preach to reinforce them. We will notice problems and address them. We will recognize that some truths cannot be received until certain fears or sins are faced (John 16:12). We will observe areas of ignorance and supply what is lacking. We will balance the diet, including doctrine, rebuke, correction, and training in righteousness in proportions that achieve the purpose for which we preach – thorough equipping that makes the church ready for any good work.

# 9

## Preparing Your Mind (3)

**Thinking rightly about the World, the Flesh, and the Devil**

He would be a foolish preacher who went forth to speak on behalf of God as if God had no adversaries intent upon derailing the message. Preaching is more than our communicating with people. It is God's speaking through us where both listeners and speaker are under bombardment from the world, the flesh, and the devil. These three enemies of the truth gang up on the preacher and the congregation to counteract our efforts. The world, as I use the term here and as John and Paul sometimes use it in the New Testament, is the fall-distorted thinking and acting that stands against God and his message that we preach.[1] The world makes our message sound implausible, like the sort of foolishness no one believes. Many dismiss what we say because they cannot conceive how it could possibly be true in light of what they take for granted as reality. This is formidable and pervasive opposition.

The flesh, 'that inclination of each person that remains in rebellion against God and does not submit to the Holy Spirit,' is a second obstacle in preaching.[2] Not only are our listeners to some extent resistant to the word of God; we as preachers are, too. We can resonate with the apostle Paul's anguished cry, 'What a wretched man I am! Who will deliver me from this body of death?' (Rom. 7:24). The opposition to preaching is not just external.

The third enemy of preaching is the enemy of our souls, the evil one himself. He blinds people to the truth, is the father of the lies the world believes, and accuses us in order to disqualify and

---

[1] 1 Corinthians 1:20-21. See the *New International Standard Bible Encyclopedia* (Grand Rapids: Eerdmans, 1988), Vol. 4, 114-15, for helpful discussion of the words used in Scripture for 'world'.

[2] This is not the only way the word is used in the New Testament, but it is an important usage as in Galatians 5:16-21. The NIV renders 'flesh' as 'the sinful nature' in verses 16, 17, 19.

dishearten us. He casts doubt on the word of God and misuses it as he has done from the beginning.[3] He craftily disguises himself as an angel of light and in that guise invades the church (2 Cor. 11:13-15). In fact, that is true of each of these enemies of sound preaching. They all are found operating in the midst of the church.

A *foolish* preacher ignores the world, the flesh, and the devil. An *unbelieving* one surrenders to them or lets them chain God's word. Yet, for every weapon used against us we have others that are stronger. As Paul put it:

> For though we live in the world, we do not wage war as the world does. The weapons we fight with are not the weapons of the world. On the contrary, they have divine power to demolish strongholds. We demolish arguments and every pretension that sets itself up against the knowledge of God, and we take captive every thought to make it obedient to Christ (2 Cor. 10:3-5).

What are those divinely powerful weapons? First and foremost is the presence of God himself, in whose name we preach. David's defeat of Goliath was a foregone conclusion, given the reality of his bold words: 'You come against me with sword and spear and javelin, but I come against you in the name of the LORD Almighty, the God of the armies of Israel whom you have defied' (1 Sam. 17:45; see also verses 26, 37, 43, 47). Samuel's word came to all Israel precisely because the Lord was with him (1 Sam. 3:19–4:1). The Lord made young Jeremiah into 'a fortified city, an iron pillar and a bronze wall' to stand against the whole land (Jer. 1:18). He gave him his word, and watched over him to see that it was fulfilled. He also promised, 'I am with you and will rescue you' (Jer. 1:19). Even Ezekiel, who knew ahead of time that his rebellious listeners would not heed God's word, knew that the Spirit was guiding him and that the strong hand of the Lord was upon him (Ezek. 2:1-15). The Lord Jesus promises to be with all those who make disciples by teaching them to obey all his commands (Matt. 28:20). When Jesus himself confronts the devil,

---

[3]E.g., Genesis 3:1, 'Did God really say ...?'; and Genesis 3:3, where he adds to God's statement. See also Matthew 4:6.

he does not face him 'toe to toe'. Jesus' *feet* crush Satan's *head* (Eph. 1:19-23). The Holy Spirit who indwells us also leads us and enables us to put to death the misdeeds of the body, to crucify the flesh, and to discern the folly of the world.[4]

Second, we have the cross. The saints ultimately overcome the devil, the accuser of the brethren, 'by the blood of the Lamb and by the word of their testimony' (Rev. 12:7-12). Jesus triumphed over the powers by the cross in history, in time, and in eternity (Col. 2:15). Our triumph is in him.

Third, we have the whole armor of God that enables us to stand against all demonic forces of whatever rank. Included in the panoply is the word of God, which is the sword of the Spirit (Eph. 6:10-18). Preaching itself, like a sword, is both an offensive and defensive weapon. We preach the word both to 'encourage others by sound doctrine, and refute those who oppose it' (Titus 1:9). What makes this armor effective is that it is *God's* armor, not ours. These weapons are only effective, however, when we use them.

Fourth, we have prayer. In Ephesians 6, in the context of the spiritual battle, Paul specifically requests prayer for his preaching. He asks that 'a word be given to him in the opening of his mouth with boldness'. He recognizes that in light of God's power he should speak boldly despite the nature of his adversaries. So he invites friends to ask God that it would be so (Eph. 6:19-20).

Do you see why Paul said his weapons were divine and powerful? All the weapons that enable us to preach faithfully, despite the world, the flesh, and the devil, are centered in the Triune God. He himself assures our victory by his life in us and for us. If we wait to recall these dynamics until the week we intend to preach, it will be too late. God calls us to walk with him day by day so that we may be ready to speak for him when he opens a door for the word. Peter captures the connection between what we have and what we are to do:

---

[4] Romans 8:13; Galatians 5: 24; 1 Corinthians 2:14-16. See Paul E. Brown, *The Holy Spirit and the Bible: The Spirit's Interpreting Role in Relation to Biblical Hermeneutics* (Fearn, Scotland: Mentor/Christian Focus Publications, 2002), 95.

His divine power has given us everything we need for life and godliness through our knowledge of him who called us by his own glory and goodness. Through these he has given us his very great and precious promises, so that through them you may participate in the divine nature and escape the corruption in the world caused by evil desires. For this very reason, make every effort to add to your faith goodness; and to your goodness, knowledge; and to knowledge, self control; and to self control, perseverance; and to perseverance, godliness; and to godliness, brotherly kindness; and to brotherly kindness, love. For if you possess these qualities in increasing measure, they will keep you from being ineffective and unproductive in your knowledge of our Lord Jesus Christ (2 Pet. 1:3-8).

## Thinking rightly about success

Just about everyone wants to succeed. That is true of preachers and prospective preachers. We want to do well. I want to succeed. I hope you do. But not everyone has the same definition of success, even when it comes to preaching. Some beginning preachers just want to survive the experience and avoid making fools of themselves. Some want their listeners to like them or to invite them to preach at another time. Some want to develop a reputation as a good speaker or a powerful communicator. There is a place for the approval of our listeners. The apostle Paul intentionally spoke so as to commend himself to everyone's conscience in the sight of God (2 Cor. 4:2). He did not want to employ unworthy techniques in preaching or to distort the message lest his preaching not be self-authenticating in hearts where God was already at work. That kind of approval has a place. Unfortunately, congregations include people with itching ears who just want the preacher to say what they want to hear; we mustn't let *them* define success. It is God's approval that matters most, and therefore it is his definition of success we should adopt.

When we consider others who have evidently been called to speak for God, we discover that success is not always defined in terms of observable, immediate results. Moses and Aaron spoke for God, but Pharaoh did not repent. Despite that lack of repentance,

God made certain that the Egyptians knew that he was the LORD (Exod. 7:3-5). Isaiah was commissioned to go with a discouraging message that his listeners would not hear and he was to preach it until their cities were ruined and their land was utterly forsaken (Isa. 6:9-13). Nevertheless, God preserved a holy seed and ultimately achieved his purposes. Jeremiah preached for decades to a rebellious people who would not listen to him, who ridiculed and mocked him. His assessment of life as a preacher was: 'Whenever I speak, I cry out proclaiming violence and destruction. So the word of the Lord has brought me insult and reproach all day long' (Jer. 20:8). That does not sound like what most people call success, but generations later when people were asked who they reckoned Jesus was, they thought first of Jeremiah (Matt. 16:14). When Ezekiel spoke for God he knew he could anticipate mixed results in his rebellious hearers but a certain, worthwhile outcome from God's viewpoint. 'And whether they listen or fail to listen –for they are a rebellious house – they will know that a prophet has been among them' (Ezek. 2:5).

In the New Testament, the apostle Paul was beaten and left for dead outside Lystra. Nevertheless, he got up and kept on preaching, winning large numbers of disciples (Acts 14:19-21). He regarded success in terms of the progress of the word of God and of the gospel, not his own circumstances (2 Tim. 2:9, Phil. 1:12-14). The apostle John spent some of his last years exiled on a barren island. Nevertheless, he is called Christ's servant, and those who read his prophecy, and who hear it and take it to heart are blessed.

Success in preaching is speaking for God in such a way that God's voice sounds forth. Sometimes his words will be heeded; often they will not. We can pray that they will be received and put no obstacle in their way, but we cannot open deaf ears or blind eyes. It may help to think of success in preaching in terms of four aspirations: faithfulness, clarity, sensitivity to the situation, and anointing by the Holy Spirit. The order of these four aspirations is intentional. If we are not faithful to the message we have received, clarity and sensitivity are beside the point. A clear but false message is worse than worthless, no matter how carefully targeted. If we achieve faithfulness and clarity but disregard the situation of our listeners, we will be speaking into the air. We may succeed at the first three aspirations – faithfulness, clarity and sensitivity – but unless the Holy Spirit breathes life into the words they will not give life to our hearers. So let us consider these in more detail.

First, success in preaching requires multifaceted faithfulness. That begins with faithfulness *to the text of Scripture*. What we say for God should be what God has said for himself. Our messages must be faithful to the words, grammar, and syntax of the text, its content *and* intent, its genre, tone, and contexts (literary, historical, theological). We even need to be faithful to what the text says between the lines and does *not* say.

But it is not just to the text itself that we must be faithful. We are called to be faithful to the passage *theologically*. That is, we are to be true to what the whole Bible is seeking to convey, and so read each passage in light of the whole. Our messages are to conform to the pattern of sound doctrine (1 Tim. 1:10; 6:3; 2 Tim. 1:13; 4:3). For instance, we will always preach in the light of the certainty of the return of Christ, even when expounding texts that do not mention the Second Coming. Our sermons will always articulate accurate biblical anthropology, describing people the way they really are. Our messages will reflect biblical proportions, emphasizing what the Bible underscores and leaving as secondary what is peripheral.

Further, we are to be faithful *spiritually*. Our messages should be true to what the Bible teaches about how people grow in grace, how they are sanctified. For example, we won't expect people to make lasting changes in isolation from genuine fellowship. We will let doctrine and ethics play their proper roles, allowing the *indicatives* of Scripture (what it tells us) to pave the way for the *imperatives* (what it commands us to do). That is, we don't neglect either the truths of Scripture or its claims upon us. We don't let our messages become either mere Bible lessons or unfounded pleas for action. Instead, we root every appeal for response in the truths the text in context teaches.

Furthermore, we must strive for faithfulness *motivationally*. As Robert Murray McCheyne wrote, 'I see a man cannot be a faithful minister until he preaches Christ for Christ's sake – until he gives up striving to attract people to himself, and seeks only to attract them to Christ.'[5]

Finally, our messages must be faithful *personally*. They will ring true only if we have submitted to the Scriptures from which we are preaching and which we are seeking to obey. Faithfulness is foundational. We achieve it by the hard work of careful Bible study, detailed exegesis, and humble submission to the will of God who graciously helps us by his Spirit in answer to prayer.

Second, success in preaching requires *clarity of expression*. If faithfulness is the fruit of sanctified exegesis, clarity is the goal of sermon construction. Once we know what the message from God is, and not before, we labor to make it plain and understandable. The key is to make the sermon as plain as Scripture is. Paul wrote, 'For we do not write you anything you cannot read or understand.'[6] His letters were carefully crafted to move people to a fuller understanding and to the God-glorifying obedience that flows from seeing things from God's perspective. To achieve that goal Paul's letters had to be clear. He sought to set forth the truth plainly (2 Cor. 4:2).

How do we make our sermons plain and clear? It does not just happen. We have to work at it, and that work involves thinking, writing, editing, and practicing. Clarity of expression requires structure and form. Every sermon must be cohesive with a unity of thought, theme, and purpose. It needs to demonstrate sequential progression, some logical flow from one part to the next. Clarity is enhanced by simplicity. Clarity grows with concreteness and fades with abstraction. Learn to write in a clear *oral* style.

Third, success in preaching demands *sensitivity* to the situation. All the faithfulness you can achieve coupled with brilliant clarity can be largely wasted if you do not consider your intended audience. This requires *alertness* to what the Holy Spirit wants to say from the text he inspired to those he will gather to listen. Ask him to

---

[5]Brian Borgman, *My Heart for Thy Cause: Albert N. Martin's Theology of Preaching* (Fearn, Scotland: Mentor/Christian Focus Publications, 2002), 157.

[6]2 Corinthians 1:13. In this Paul was following the example of his Lord who said, 'I spoke openly to the world' (John 18:20).

disclose it to you for their benefit, and he will. Astonishingly, the Holy Spirit kept Paul and his co-workers from preaching the word in the province of Asia! (Acts 16:6). It took real spiritual sensitivity to discern that the time was not right to preach there because another assignment needed to come first.

Sensitivity also requires *awareness* of the flock. The good shepherd *knows* his sheep. The more you know about them and their needs, temptations, discouragements, joys, and challenges, the more likely you are to see how your text legitimately speaks to them. Sensitivity means being aware of the diversity within the congregation: differences in age, education, status, family situation, maturity, and biases, as well as differences in spiritual vitality. Sensitivity includes awareness of events in the community and the world. Only an *insensitive* pastor would have continued his series on the qualifications of elders on Sunday, September 16, 2001. Sensitivity is a fruit of love. If we really care for those to whom we speak we will work hard to say things in ways they can understand. Love also frees us as preachers to forget about ourselves. Sensitivity is not to be exercised only when preparing to preach. If we maintain eye contact while preaching we can learn a great deal about whether the word is going home to the hearts of our listeners and adjust our course accordingly.

Fourth, success in preaching requires the *anointing* of the Holy Spirit, which is to say that preparing to preach is more than technical competence, more than the sum of the parts we will list shortly. We want to stop short of saying that success in preaching involves bearing fruit, because that does not happen each time we preach. We avoid saying that successful preaching has God's blessing on it for much the same reason. Nothing we do entices God to anoint us or our preaching. Jesus is supremely the Anointed One whom God uniquely set apart for his saving work (Acts 4:26-27; 10:38). In him, God has anointed all who believe.[7] Since this anointing is something believers already have, to say that success requires the Spirit's anointing is to say that we succeed only when we expectantly invite the Holy Spirit to work in us and our listeners, illuminating,

---

[7] 2 Corinthians 1:21; 1 John 2:20, 27. See also Paul E. Brown, *The Holy Spirit and the Bible*.

teaching, convicting, and sanctifying as we prepare and speak and as we all respond. Paul tells us that he speaks as one taught by the Holy Spirit to those who by the Spirit are able to understand the gifts God has given (1 Cor. 2:12-16). The Spirit's ministry in both speaker and listener is indispensable because left to ourselves we would not listen, believe, understand, or obey. Our task is to let ourselves be taught by the Spirit as we study the Bible and seek words to express its truths. Then we place ourselves as preachers, the sermon, and every listener on the altar as living sacrifices and we invite God to send fire from heaven to ignite our hearts to speak his word and all our hearts to hear and joyfully respond to it.[8]

Success in preaching, as some define it, is not worth having. Success as God defines it is one of the great blessings of anyone called to minister the word.

---

[8]Tony Sargent, *The Sacred Anointing* (Wheaton, IL: Crossway, 1994), documents D. Martyn Lloyd-Jones' understanding of the necessity of anointed preaching.

# 10

## Preparing Your Body to Preach

Christianity is an incarnate faith. Jesus has a body that was born and grew, in which he learned obedience, died on the cross, was raised immortal, and will come again to reign, to save, and to judge. Nothing we do can compare with the uniqueness of Christ's descent into human flesh. Nevertheless, it should not strike us as odd that the message of God's love incarnate is conveyed to our listeners by us – people who have bodies. Jesus sent his apostles even as he was sent (John 20:21). 'How beautiful are the feet of those who preach the good news!' (Rom. 10:15). Though the language is poetic, the word picture recalls reality. We speak from bodies that have feet and voices. We would not be wise to preach without preparing our bodies to do so, for what people see when we preach cannot help but influence what they hear.

A surprising number of preachers in the history of the church have not been able-bodied. William Booth, founder of the Salvation Army and a tireless preacher, was warned by his doctor at the age of 26 that he would not survive a year as an evangelist. When he was thirty-three a life insurance company agreed to underwrite his life only if he paid an increased premium. He was an insomniac whose stomach was always in pain. His secretary, a major of half his age, wore a special uniform whose coat had forty-three pockets, all for items General Booth routinely needed, many of them related to his many physical ailments. Yet Booth lived to the age of eighty-three and preached powerfully to the end.[9]

If you have physical disabilities or unusual limitations, prayerfully expect God's strength to be made perfect in weakness, as Paul learned when coming to terms with his thorn in the flesh. He even said that he first preached to the Galatians *because* of a bodily ailment

---

[9]Richard Collier, *The General Next to God: The Story of William Booth and the Salvation Army* (London: Collins, 1965), 39, 218.

(Gal. 4:13). If you are strong and healthy, thank God and consecrate your body as a living sacrifice, to be poured out on the altar of the faith of your listeners. Paul tells us he beat his own body to make it his slave, so that having preached to others, the same body that preached would not do something that disqualified him for the prize (1 Cor. 9:27).

This toughness with ourselves, this going into training, is not an optional extra for preachers. We owe this to our listeners and to the Lord, for we preach not in the short-term but for the long-term as well. We do not want something we do or fail to do *later* to undermine what we have preached today. Our goal is a responsible stewardship of the bodies God has given us so they may be useful in his service as long as he is our master. That means fitness for the task. You may not be fit enough to run a marathon, but you must be physically fit enough to preach. You and I need stamina, energy, concentration, and voice. I suggest long-term and short-term strategies to protect and steward the physical assets you have been given.

In the long-term, take care of your body; build it up so you will have the necessary strength. Employ a judicious combination of exercise, moderate diet, and sufficient rest. Find some exercise that you enjoy and that is age-appropriate. It may be a vigorous regimen of weight lifting or a gentle daily stroll with your spouse. Eat slowly and enjoy God's good gifts, eating and drinking to the glory of God (1 Cor. 10:31; Rom. 14:21). Keep track of your weight without being compulsive about it, and discipline yourself to move in the direction of what is ideal for you. Many people gain about two pounds a year, and that adds up. Do you want to be 40 pounds overweight when you are 50 or 60 years old? Minimize the use of addictive drinks with dubious nutritional value, especially those with stimulants like caffeine that override your body's calls for rest and depressants like alcohol that impair your inhibitions. You may live in a place where you are grateful for every calorie you can get, and exercise is a way of life; an early bed time is dictated by the patchy availability of electricity. Some of the rest of us would do well to limit our excessive consumption of food and late-night television viewing, out of solidarity with such. Those whose bodies bespeak discipline and sacrifice find that their appearance reinforces their message. Those who are significantly overweight inevitably find listeners skeptical when they extol the virtues of self-control or describe such disciplines as fasting.

Take care of your eyes by using adequate lighting when you read and by correcting vision problems when you can. Contact lenses that achieve good vision are usually an advantage for preachers, eliminating one more barrier between us and our listeners and leaving one less thing to fiddle with as we preach.

Look after your vocal apparatus by avoiding noisy coughing and unnecessary throat clearing, yelling and screaming, conversations in noisy places such as cars and restaurants, and contact with air pollution including tobacco smoke. Drink lots of liquids – preferably not too hot nor too cold. Develop your ability to project your voice with the zeal of any athlete who wants to be able to compete and win. These muscles can be trained and strengthened; good habits can be learned. This comes mainly with practice, but you have to practice the right things! Speak to the back row, but don't shout or strain. A speech therapist, vocal coach, or well-trained choir director can help you know what to do and can spot bad habits that need to be overcome.

Don't neglect your posture. This is no small task for those of us who spend hours at our books and in unnatural positions in front of computer screens. The effort is worth the price both in terms of capacity to breathe and speak, and in appearance and ethos.

Jesus exhorts us not to worry about clothes (Matt. 6:25-33), and we should always obey him. Clearly the most important clothing is to be clothed with Christ and the virtues that come from following him (Rom. 13:14; Gal. 3:27; Col. 3:12-14). Nevertheless, seeking first his kingdom requires putting no obstacle in anyone's way even when it comes to secondary things (Rom. 14:13). This is the guiding principle when it comes to choosing what to wear when you preach. Avoid distracting people by your appearance. God can use an unusual face or plain features or even physical handicaps to get people's attention, but your goal should be to dress in such a way that you become more or less invisible so that Jesus in all his power and glory shines through. I put these thoughts in the long-term strategy section because I understand that you may need to buy shoes for your children before you supplement your own wardrobe. As you pray about these things, the Lord will supply your need.

Here are a few modest suggestions. Try to see that whatever you wear is clean, unwrinkled, and fits your body neither too tightly nor too loosely. If it is too tight, you won't be able to breathe and move; if it is too loose, you may look sloppy. Choose clothing that does not draw undue attention to you or any part of your body. If you are still on your way to your ideal weight, try to wear clothes that don't accentuate the extra pounds or your thinness. Wear the kind of shoes that don't draw attention to themselves. Let local custom inform but not dictate how formal or casual your clothing is. Your goal is not to portray yourself as 'one of the guys' or as a television talk-show host on the set in a broadcast studio. You are here to speak for the living God. If your tradition calls for wearing distinctive clerical attire, make sure it is clean, pressed, and in good repair. Make sure that what shows below it doesn't make a mockery of it. If you don't have clothes that seem suitable, ask the Lord to supply them. You may be surprised to discover that you can find better quality clothes in second-hand or thrift shops, and at a fraction of the price, than what you can afford to buy new. If you are blessed with adequate resources, buy one well-made, classic, quality outfit instead of two or three cheaper, trendier sets of clothes. It will stay in style longer and look better each time you wear it. A different tie or shirt or other accessory can supply necessary variety.

Just a word to the wise about grooming: don't neglect it. Most people will look at you while you preach. Try not to make the experience distracting or distressing. Men, consider foregoing wearing of facial hair. It hides part of your countenance, making it more difficult for people to see your expressions. If you do wear a moustache or beard, keep it trimmed along with other unwanted hair. If you shave, do so. Keep your hair clean and get a haircut well before people notice you need it. Women, make sure your hair is arranged so that you don't have to push it away from your face every few moments. This can be a distracting mannerism.

What then is your *short-term strategy* for physical fitness for preaching? Simply employ the long-term strategy every day. Just make sure that, if possible, you are rested and that you do not eat a large meal just before you preach. You want your blood to go to your head, not to your stomach, and you don't want to be dealing with gases released during digestion when you are trying to speak. Have a room-temperature glass of water available. Relax and trust God. Check your clothing to make sure every part is where it should be and functioning as it should. Then forget about yourself and think about the glories of the word of God and the needs of your hearers.

# 11

## Preparing the Congregation to Hear and Obey God's Word

Preaching is much more than communication, but it is not less. Communication does not happen until someone receives the message conveyed. Our responsibility as preachers is to prepare ourselves to preach. But we will be wise if we also prepare our listeners to hear. We have already seen that not all listeners are the same. Not every listener in a church or parachurch meeting has the capacity to receive the meat of the word (1 Pet. 2:2; Heb. 5:11-14). But every responsible leader in either setting wants more of the listeners to be able to receive more of the word as time passes. How do we facilitate that? How do we help Christians develop a hunger for meaty, health-giving preaching? We can't *make* people listen, but we can and must do our part to *prepare* them to listen. How do we do that?

First, we acknowledge with gratitude to God that some people *are* prepared to listen. The Holy Spirit has prepared them to receive the word (1 Thess. 1:2–2:14). They show by the fruit of their lives that they have 'ears to hear' (Mark 4:1-20). In addition, there are often other reasons why they continue to feed on the word. For instance, they have accurate expectations of what should happen when the word is preached. They expect to hear from God, to be encouraged, built up, sanctified, established in their faith, challenged, rebuked, corrected and trained in righteousness. So they listen with humble anticipation (Acts 10:33; James 1:21). They know enough of the Word to listen actively, to test all things and hold fast to that which is good (1 Thess. 5:21). They have prayed for illumination, that they might be taught, and might have understanding (Ps. 119:18, 66, 135, 144, 169). They know that reconciliation with others precedes communion with God (Matt. 5: 23-24), and that extending forgiveness to those who have sinned against them is the precondition of receiving forgiveness from the One against whom they have sinned

(Matt. 6:14-15). They see themselves as humble servants awaiting a word from their Master that they might faithfully obey it. Because they hunger and thirst for righteousness, they open wide their mouths that God would fill them (Matt. 5:6; Ps. 80:10). Ideally, such listeners are physically fit and rested. They are neither hungry nor overfed so that their own bodies don't distract them from the hard work of listening. Such people will always be a major means God uses to challenge others to listen to his word. Their love for him will be contagious as it was in the case of the Thessalonians. As preachers we rejoice in such people, affirm them, and let their examples spur others on to follow Christ as they do.

There will be others, however, who do not listen. The wise preacher will discern that they fail to hear the preached word for a variety of reasons and will treat each hindrance appropriately. Some, as we have already noted, are *not able to hear*. They are spiritually dead and need to be raised with Christ. They are blind and need their eyes opened. They do not have ears to hear and need to receive them. The veil still covers their eyes whenever Scripture is read. Only when such people turn to the Lord is the veil taken away (2 Cor. 3:14-16). Our task with respect to them is to keep on proclaiming the gospel, knowing that the Holy Spirit uses the word of God to bring about rebirth (James 1:18), and to pray that their eyes would be opened.

Then there are those who could hear but *do not want to hear*. They are regenerate but in some degree of rebellion. Isaiah 30:9-11 describes them well:

> These are rebellious people, deceitful children, children unwilling to listen to the LORD's instruction. They say to the seers 'See no more visions!' and to the prophets, 'Give us no more visions of what is right! Tell us pleasant things, prophesy illusions. Leave this way, get off this path, and stop confronting us with the Holy One of Israel!'

The context makes it plain that their trust was misplaced. They relied upon their own strategies instead of God. By contrast, those who wait for the LORD will be able to hear (30:21; 32:3). The Lord Jesus makes it plain that this hindrance to listening did not automatically vanish with his arrival. In John 7:17 he prescribes the remedy: 'If anyone chooses to do God's will, he will find out whether my teaching comes from God or whether I speak on my own.' Willingness to obey precedes ability to understand God's word.

There are also some who do not listen because in one way or another *they see themselves as being above God's word*, instead of in humble submission to it. They may see it as merely a tool, a resource to help them achieve their personal or professional goals. They may treat it as a justification for the way they already act or believe instead of seeing it as a normative revelation from God that critiques and corrects all individuals and all cultures. Sadly, some even treat it as a stick with which to beat other people into submission. These people only hear the parts of the word that reinforce their previously held beliefs. They do not really listen to it. We who preach to such people may need to administer Paul's rhetorical question, 'Did the word of God originate with you? Or are you the only people it has reached?' (1 Cor. 14:36). We all need humbly to accept the word that has been planted in us (James 1:21). Only when we have given our bodies as living sacrifices and have let our minds be renewed are we able to test and approve God's will (Rom. 12:1-2).

Another category of people who do not listen as they should includes *those who have not responded to what they have already heard*. These may be some of the hardest to detect in the church because their notebooks are full of spiritual insights from sermons and studies but their lives fall short of transformation. They take in ideas, but they do not produce fruit. The Lord Jesus spoke of such people as being like the man who built his house on the sand in contrast to the one who built on the rock. Jesus says that both builders 'hear these words of mine.' The difference is that one puts the words into practice; the other does not (Matt. 7:24-27). James says the same thing even more directly in 1:22-25:

'Do not merely listen to the word and so deceive yourselves. Do what it says. Anyone who listens to the word but does not do what it says is like a man who looks at his face in the mirror and, after looking at himself goes away and immediately forgets what he looks like. But the man who looks intently into the perfect law that gives freedom, and continues to do this, not forgetting what he has heard, but doing it – he will be blessed in what he does.'

James' words remind us how we can prepare people to listen by the way we preach. Every message aims for obedience; but every message gives freedom. To put it another way, no text of Scripture is irrelevant for life. All Scripture is God-breathed and profitable. But not every text is a rebuke or a correction. Not every passage tells us something else we must be or do. Many texts remind us of God's mercy and grace, of his patience and faithfulness. Indeed, in its larger context every passage offers good news – even if its immediate purpose is to remind us how much we need it. So if we want to help people hear the Bible, we preach the Bible so that listeners will know what is required of them and know the grace of God that is available to help them do what is asked. We will want to preach so that people are not crushed by a load that neither we nor they could ever bear. That was the way of the Pharisees (Matt. 23:1-4). Instead, we point to specific steps of obedience, baby steps, steps that may be taken by faith and in the power of the Holy Spirit by those who humbly receive the teaching. And if we are wise, we do not hurriedly rush to the next topic with more stated or implied duties. We give the Spirit time to shape the listeners with the word. We know that until our listeners have taken the first steps, they are not ready for the second and third ones.

The challenge here is to avoid two perils: implying either that the way of obedience is solely our doing or, on the other hand, that it is entirely God's work. Because we know that 'it is God who works in us both to will and to act according to his good purpose' (Phil 2:13), we exhort people to obey, to work out their salvation with fear and trembling. That is why we urge people to 'trust *and* obey,' not 'trust *or* obey.' It is also why we pray. A wonderful model prayer is reported in Colossians 1:9-12 where Paul tells the Colossians how he has been praying for them. They had already heard the gospel and were bearing fruit and growing. Paul asks God to fill them with the knowledge of his will through all spiritual wisdom and understanding. That is a major aim of preaching. But Paul's prayer is that this knowledge, wisdom, and understanding would be purposeful. Hear what he prays next: 'And we pray this in order that you may live a life worthy of the Lord and may please him in every way: bearing fruit in every good work, *growing in the knowledge of God.*' Notice the last phrase. Between initial knowledge and growing knowledge is obedient living. If our preaching helps our listeners obey, it will help them continue to listen. If on the other hand, we make it more difficult for them to obey, we share responsibility for their declining ability to hear.

A closely related hindrance in hearing is that *some listeners can't hear because their diet does not match their maturity.* The writer to the Hebrews lamented that his readers were not ready for solid food. Like babies, they could not chew and digest the meat of the word so they needed to start all over again with milk. Nevertheless, he is eager to press on with them beyond the basics (Heb. 5:11-6:3). We who preach have a responsibility to see to it that the messages we preach feed the listeners we have. We can't help them grow if they cannot digest what we as stewards of God's word bring from the kitchen to the table. To be sure, maturity comes from 'constant use' of the truth, as we have just seen, but our responsibility remains. Some spiritual babies have failed to grow because they have been offered steak before they have cut their teeth. But, in my judgment, more growing Christians have been stunted by preachers who offer milk long after babies should be given meat. In practice, both spiritual infants and mature saints – and many in between – will be in every healthy church. So if we want everyone to listen we will make sure that each message reaffirms some basic truths and also stretches the more mature. Like the loving parent, we will put nourishing food in digestible portions before the young while giving the growing young adults in the faith something they can sink their teeth into.

Another group of would-be listeners have simply gotten in *the habit of not listening.* Some of these people think they already know all that the preacher will say and, sadly, sometimes their attitude is justified. The preacher has not thought deeply or read widely and the message *is* entirely predictable. Others are put off by the form of the message. It may strike them as too logical, or not orderly enough; too serious, not serious enough; too long or too short. Here again, their excuses may be all too understandable. But for whatever reason, the rewards for listening do not seem to repay the effort. Having not been fed recently, they see no reason to expect a meal this Sunday. How do you help such folk gain or regain a good appetite? The remedy, I suggest, is to offer good teaching about preaching, combined with good examples of preaching, reinforced by other opportunities to develop a taste for the Bible. In this threefold strategy, where you start matters less than that you work at all three. Some habitual non-listeners will develop a hunger for good preaching by starting with meaningful private Bible study or by being in a good growth group. Some may gain a taste for good preaching by being individually discipled or by reading a book that opens up the Bible to them or helps them see the benefits of knowing and living it. Others will get excited when they hear someone expound a text of Scripture that was unclear or irrelevant to them before they heard it well preached. Still others will need to have their expectations clarified and heightened by a more formal explanation of what the Bible is for and how preaching uses it – the very kinds of ideas we have pursued so far in this book. Such teaching might be part of a membership class that orients people who are new to the church. There you can explain what they should expect when you expound the Bible in church.

The key ingredient in this recipe is your own preaching. Your excitement about the message you have seen in the Bible will be contagious. Make each message digestible and appetizing without watering it down. Pray and work hard at it. Enlist friends to give you candid feedback. Model right handling of the word of God, every time you open it. The Bible itself will often be the tool God uses to stir people up. A direct and vivid rebuke of Laodicean lukewarmness may be called for.

A growing number of those who come to church can't seem to hear the preacher because they are *listening to other voices*. I include in this category all those who are type- three soil in Jesus' parable. 'Still others, like seed sown among thorns, hear the word;

but the worries of this life, the deceitfulness of wealth and the desires for other things come in and choke the word, making it unfruitful' (Mark 4:18-19). Technically, these people are hearers, but practically they are not. Their minds are preoccupied with grocery lists and soccer schedules, with the stock market and the board meeting, with the latest fashion or newest media celebrity. Their ambitions arise not from the word but from the world. When they sit still for a moment in church, the siren call of this present age still beckons and its sheer volume and appeal easily drown the lone voice in the pulpit. Or perhaps the concerns of this life are darker and more sinister. Fears, regrets, guilt, and discouragement render them pessimistic about the future and even about God's ability to rescue them from their own folly and sin.

It is in this context that the counsel of James 4 is especially helpful. There, friendship with the world is overcome by humble submission to God who opposes the proud but gives grace to the humble. 'Come near to God and he will come near to you. Wash your hands you sinners, and purify your hearts, you double-minded' (4:8). This is why the preaching of the word is best received in the context of genuine worship. We are never to worship God as a means to an end, but when we intentionally come into his presence, he meets with us and helps us set aside our love for the world. The worshiper who pours out his or her heart to God is more likely to be ready to have it filled with God's word. Preparing our listeners to hear God's voice includes meaningful expressions of *corporate* confession in worship. This helps us all acknowledge that when ignorance and instability characterize us we will be much more likely to distort the Scriptures to our own destruction (2 Pet. 3:16). Candor in the pulpit can be a less threatening way to help people hear what Scripture is actually saying. For example, we may confess, 'For a long time I was unable to receive this teaching. Perhaps that was because it forces me to admit my own guilt. I constructed an elaborate means to explain this away.' Then we describe our former defensive or distorted interpretation of the text at hand and show how that was rooted in our faulty thinking and living. By doing that, others may see themselves and be convicted and corrected. We as preachers cannot weed the garden of someone else's heart, but we can point out the weeds and urge our hearers to root them out, dig them out, or starve them out. And we can set before them the beautiful and abundant fruit that comes from a well-weeded garden.

Others who cannot hear the word because they are listening to other voices are those who are listening not merely to the common enticements of the world, but instead are taken up with a more intellectual worldliness. Their failure to hear and heed Scripture arises from a very different view of the world. They don't hear what you preach because their biases, training, and experience incline them to come to the sermon in a very different way. They see themselves in the driver's seat with the text of Scripture as merely a prompt to elicit their own thoughts which they consider definitive, or at least as valid as anyone else's, including the preacher's. For these folks, the Bible does not *speak*, it merely *reflects*. Therefore, in their minds they do not submit to it; they evaluate it. Instead of feeding upon it, they treat it as a picky eater would a sumptuous buffet. They look for something they like and leave the rest.

Others may rule out some clearly-taught truths because of intellectual commitments that discount the supernatural. Still others may import numerology or some equally faulty interpretive approach that is utterly foreign to the text of Scripture. Some have invested themselves heavily in cultic or otherwise heterodox teachings and find it difficult to let the Bible have the last word on those ideas. Others operate from a rule- or shame-based mindset that colors everything they hear the preacher say.

These factors affect not merely those who are *evidently* suppressing the truth by their wickedness (Rom. 1:18-32; Eph. 4:18-19), but all of us to some extent, because the renewing of our minds is not yet complete. We have to acknowledge humbly our own biases and invite the Holy Spirit to see to it that the Bible first speaks to us, rebuking our sins and shortcomings, and then correcting us by its truth. The better pastors we are, the more we will know about the real struggles and distorted ideas of our parishioners. Knowing them, we can address them.

Your weapon of choice in countering faulty thinking is the word of God that you proclaim. Remember that a crucial part of preaching is getting below the surface of the text. Let it address presuppositions that keep your listeners from receiving its truth. For instance, let's say you are expounding 1 Timothy 6:6-19 and want to drive home the truth that *the love of money is not easy to root out; it takes a radical reorientation called 'repentance'.* You do not merely exhort people to stop loving money. Instead, you help them see four radical adjustments in thought and life that the text brings to light. Verses 6-8 describe a *redefinition of what is profitable.* Verses 12, 13 and 19 offer a *re-evaluation of what is truly life.* Verses 13-19 call for a *re-affirmation of God's character and plan.* Verses 11-12, 17-19 command a *redirection from earthly values to heavenly ones.* Your message will call for action, but it will be solidly rooted in good theology and a biblical worldview. There may be many reasons people persist in loving money, but among them are surely faulty presuppositions about what is profitable, what life really is, who God is, and what his plan is, not to mention the value of eternity. We will never help people listen to God's word until we get down to the level where they (perhaps unconsciously) resist it. It also pays to put good books in people's hands. Print can address substantive issues more thoroughly than is usually possible in oral discourse. Engage people in meaningful conversation that helps them see where their minds still need renewing.

Yet another group of people do not hear because of *external distractions.* Babies cry or the room is too hot or too cold, and concentration deteriorates. Invariably, someone coughs, or the sound amplification system begins to whine, or a distracting person enters one's field of view, or a noisy vehicle passes by. The possibilities are almost endless. You won't be able to eliminate all distractions, but you can make progress when you fight the battle for attention on all fronts. First, enlist everyone to help minimize these distractions, especially those who can make a difference whether directly or indirectly. Encourage those who look after the church building to make sure that whatever temperature controls you are blessed with are working properly. Slightly cool is usually better than too warm.

If you have a sound system, make sure the operators have tested and retested everything, and replaced batteries preemptively. Have ushers seat people in places they reckon will maximize attention to the worship leaders and preacher. Encourage parents to discern when their child is distracting other worshipers and listeners and suggest strategies to engage the child or seek a less disruptive location. Second, ask God to give you discernment to know when you have not been heard. Maybe a baby's cry masked an important phrase and you need to repeat yourself. Sometimes your own visual aids split people's attention. The congregation fails to hear what you say because they were concentrating on the projection screen. Above all, take seriously your responsibility to hold people's attention and to make yourself heard and understood. This is an escalating challenge since a significant proportion of listeners have some measurable hearing loss. With an aging population in many countries and pervasive youthful auditory abuse, the percentage may well rise.

I realize that what makes this preparing of listeners so challenging is that it may seem like a vicious circle. Listeners are caught up in faulty thinking. The antidote to faulty thinking is clear scriptural teaching. Because of their faulty thinking, listeners are unable to receive the scriptural teaching that would correct their wrong ideas, renew their minds and transform their lives. This would indeed be vicious were it not for the promised ministry of the Holy Spirit using the word to give life and introduce light. We preach with hope in the confidence that God himself can and will do what a mere human word could never do. He opens blind eyes and unstops deaf ears; and he raises the dead. When that happens, the word becomes precious and people hunger for it. This is the Lord's doing and is marvelous in our eyes.

# Part Four:

# Preparing the Message
# God Gives You to Preach

# 12

# Preparing the Message: An Overview

So far, we have laid some foundations by setting forth a definition of preaching, noting how God himself prepares us to preach, and how despite his investment in us and presence with us, we still need to prepare. In Part Two we considered how we prepare *ourselves* to preach. In Part Three, we considered how we prepare our minds, bodies, and our *listeners* to hear and heed God's word. Now, we discuss how to prepare *the message* itself so that it is faithful, clear and sensitive to our listeners, a message the Holy Spirit might anoint. Here is a bird's eye view of this process. Preparing a message involves doing certain things, set out here for the sake of clarity as discrete steps, all of which are to be bathed in prayer.

Prayerfully,

1. Select a text of Scripture, also called a preaching portion.

2. Read the text carefully and repeatedly.

3. Study the text; that is, engage in exegesis.

4. Meditate on the text.

5. Summarize the thrust of the text in a single sentence.

6. Discern how this text speaks to your listeners. Write out a provisional proposition, that is, the thrust of the passage as it relates to your listeners.

7. Structure your message in a way that reflects how the text is designed to achieve its God-given purposes. Describe how your message will develop the proposition by means of an organizational sentence.

8. Write an outline that fulfills the promises implied by the proposition and the organizational sentence.

9. Develop each thought in the outline by anchoring it to part of the text, validating the connection, explaining it, illustrating it, and applying it.

10. Write the conclusion to the message, including, as appropriate, a final prayer.
11. Write the introduction to the message.
12. Write out the message in detail in good oral style.
13. Reduce the manuscript to notes.
14. Rehearse the sermon aloud until you are relatively free from your notes and can forget about yourself when preaching.

Experienced preachers will find that a number of these steps become automatic or are combined with others. On occasion, a flash of insight as you study the text may get you started somewhere in the middle of this list and you will work your way to the edges. As any part of the preparation process leads you to greater clarity, you will revise earlier conclusions. If you are a beginner, or if you recognize that your methodology has become sloppy, you may find it helpful to use these items the way a wise pilot uses a preflight checklist to avoid omitting something vital. A sermon can fail to get off the ground, or worse, may crash and burn, when just *one* of these items is neglected.

As we put flesh on this skeleton, your own presuppositions about preaching – and mine – will undoubtedly come to light. You may have practices or preferences that I implicitly or explicitly criticize or seem to ignore. What I set before you is not the *only* way to prepare to preach, but it is *one* way that, other things being equal, will *reduce* the likelihood of messages that are *un*faithful, *un*clear, and *in*sensitive to the congregation. I am *not* saying, 'Follow this pattern, take these steps, and you will succeed.' I *am* encouraging you to ask the Lord to use these thoughts as part of his long-term work of equipping you for the work of ministry, especially this ministry of the word we call preaching. I am trusting that he will answer your prayers.

# 13

# Submitting to the Text

## 1. Select a Text of Scripture

The little one-letter word, the article 'a' in the heading, demands some explanation. You may never have heard a message that attempted to expound a single text of Scripture, and if you have, you may have been disappointed. Isn't our task to bring to bear what the whole Bible teaches on a certain subject, or at least use a few passages to reinforce what one passage is getting at?

To answer that question, we need to remember how we got our Bibles in the form we have them. Obviously they were translated from the original languages in which they were penned, but the other major change from the original manuscripts is that they were broken into chapters and verses that were numbered for easier reference. This has been very helpful for study and recall. It obscures the fact, however, that the Bible was given to us as books which correspond (with a few exceptions) to the books named in our English Bibles. These books in turn are part of larger sections of the Bible such as the Pentateuch in the Old Testament or the Gospels in the New. These books, much less the big chunks of Scripture of which they make up the parts, don't easily lend themselves to being preached in their entirety in one sermon; there is just too much to grasp and apply.

The fact that we received the Bible in these units, some longer than others, should bias us towards trying to make known to our listeners what the original authors were trying to convey by the *books* they wrote, not merely by individual sentences, paragraphs and chapters. Evangelical Christians believe that every word of Scripture is God-breathed. That doesn't mean that we preach every word of every book in order, though in some parts of the Bible, such as the epistles, we may come close to doing so. It does mean that, whatever size text we select, we have to take seriously every word and paragraph and chapter as it contributes to the whole message of the particular book. We must also bear in mind how that book fits into its Testament and ultimately the whole Bible.

Alongside this common-sense observation, we recall that because the Bible speaks with one voice and does not contradict itself, what it *truly* teaches in one place will not disagree with what it teaches elsewhere. In fact, other passages that genuinely speak to the same subject will inform, clarify, reinforce, balance, and limit what the text we choose to expound teaches. We do not want wrongly to restrict our *study* to a single passage of Scripture when others will help us understand it.

On the other hand, putting together a coherent message that is demonstrably drawn from multiple passages has some disadvantages that need to be carefully weighed before we attempt it.

First, it may tempt us to use passages we haven't really studied as carefully as when we focus on a single text. In order to reinforce their conclusions, young preachers sometimes gather passages whose meaning, in context, they haven't really grasped.

A second disadvantage is that developing a message from a collection of passages selected by the preacher, leaves a lot to the judgment of the preacher, judgment which may or may not be good. It may be the case that another passage does actually address the topic you are trying to explain. On the other hand, the additional passages may have only limited application to your subject. Inferences drawn from them should be given less weight in the preacher's argument. Their inclusion would not strengthen the preacher's argument but weaken it. Seasoned preachers are therefore more likely to succeed at synthesizing the message of multiple passages as they address a single subject.

A third disadvantage to multiple-text preaching is that it models a way of handling of the Bible that is open to abuse. It takes time to explain why a second or third text is introduced and how its context makes the interpretation valid and the application warranted. Some listeners inevitably pick up connections but don't see why they are valid – if they are. Instead of learning how to read the Bible as a cohesive message, and letting it speak in a normal way, they get the impression that it is a sort of grab bag of isolated thoughts for the benefit of those who can draw them out of the hat and string them together.

For the above reasons, I recommend that by all means you read and *study* other texts and think about how they shed light on the one you are expounding, but that your default approach is to *expound* books of the Bible sequentially, letting texts from other places – indeed the whole Bible – help you understand your chosen text. Cite them carefully and sparingly, giving priority to explaining what the text before you is actually saying and what response it seeks and why. There will be times when citing another text is a must, but a methodology that *begins* by looking for related passages to read to your listeners in order to explain your text is a recipe for superficiality and diffusion, making its case by the cumulative weight of other witnesses instead of listening carefully to what a text is actually teaching.

By what criteria, then, do we decide how much of a Bible book we are going to expound so that people can understand it and respond to God who speaks through it? Criteria can be divided into three categories: characteristics of the text itself, your relation to the text, and the needs of your listeners.[1]

## Characteristics of the text itself

The most important thing to remember is that the text you preach must be a *unit of thought*. To preach only a phrase or other part of a sentence is a veritable invitation to transgress the author's intention and to say what *you* want to say as opposed to letting him speak. A sentence is a unit of thought and can occasionally be preached, as John 3:16 has been since the first century. Nevertheless, thoughts that are so compactly expressed tempt the preacher to develop them from other sources. Again, it is the preacher who selects these instead of letting the inspired author supply the development of the thought.

---

[1] In the epilogue, I will be saying more about developing sermon series that balance the spiritual diet of your listeners. There I will also comment on what to do if your text is selected for you by a lectionary. The material in this chapter focuses on the choice of texts for individual messages, although there is inevitably some overlap with what I will say there.

Normally a paragraph is a good starting place because there is a single thought, expressed or implied by the topic sentence of the paragraph, together with other statements that in some way explain, limit, apply, or otherwise relate to that thought. But a paragraph may not be enough text if several contiguous paragraphs all speak to the same subject and address various facets of it. In some narrative sections, we may be wise to expound several chapters together if they tell a single story that consists of a few episodes, all of which are crucial to the meaning of the whole account. You may find it valuable when preaching from the New Testament to begin with the sections set out in the United Bible Societies' edition of the Greek New Testament. They often include more than one paragraph, but only paragraphs that advance a single theme. Begin to work through the fourteen steps we will be suggesting. You may, in some cases, discover that the text you selected says far more than can be faithfully expounded on a single occasion. On other occasions, you may feel a need to go elsewhere for more material to develop the thought of your text – when in fact the development is right there in the context, but you had unwisely excluded it by selecting a preaching portion that was too small and therefore did not include it.

Other clues that will alert you to the start of a new unit of thought include place or time notations (e.g. 1 Sam. 6:1; 7:2; 8:1), introduction of new characters in a narrative (e.g. 1 Sam. 9:1), or an obvious change of subject (1 Sam. 17:1). None of these guarantees that you are in a new unit of thought, although they may signal it. Moreover, the fact that there is a chapter division at some point does not necessarily signal a separate thought or sermon.

Many cases of sermonic confusion can be solved right here. Sermons should be about one subject and should develop that subject in a way that is true to the text and edifying to listeners. Selecting a text that treats one subject and develops it with sufficient completeness is a good start. Ask the Lord to lead you to the right sized text and you will be on your way to expounding the Bible in ways that let it speak for itself.

## Your relation to the text

This second category of criteria is important because God has a way of bringing to our attention texts that need to be expounded to the people we serve. When he has a message for them, he often wants us to hear it first and respond to it. As you read the Bible personally and privately, some parts of it will speak to you more loudly than others, getting your attention, arousing your curiosity, convicting, and challenging you. They might start the wheels turning for a series you will preach in six months or a year. Obviously, this presupposes that you are feeding on the Bible and letting it speak to you. Although all sorts of reading plans have value, I recommend a plan that takes you through the Bible at least once a year, preferably one that lets you read several chapters from one part of the Bible at a sitting as opposed to reading one chapter from each of several sections every day. The advantage of this is that you are more likely to notice themes and repetitions when you focus on one book at a time. You can alternate between Old and New Testament books and read different kinds of biblical literature at different paces. I read several chapters of Old Testament narrative daily, but may take a New Testament epistle more slowly. Taking some notes and keeping track of insights by marking your Bible will provide a seed bed for further development later.

## The needs of your listeners

There is no substitute for knowing the flock. If you are a guest speaker, unfamiliar with your anticipated audience, you can ask those who do know them what sort of needs they perceive. This is a worthwhile exercise even if the answer you receive is somewhat vague. All of us have a range of spiritual needs and can benefit from the exposition of any text of Scripture. If you have a choice in the matter, you will want to expound a text that connects with your listeners by addressing a subject that concerns them, that answers questions they are asking, or feeds them in a way that balances their diet. Try to discover what ethical or relational temptations they face and what fears are common. Select a text that addresses these concerns either directly or indirectly.

One way to do this is to ask what books of the Bible were written to people whose life situation was analogous to the life situation of your listeners. For instance, the Apocalypse of John originally encouraged those under the oppressive rule of Rome and still speaks hope to those who feel utterly dominated by tyrannical regimes.[2] If they have a crying need and you ignore it, your listeners may get the impression that the Bible does not speak to life as they experience it. If the community of which they are a part is facing an issue, such as racial tension, we must be alert in our own Bible reading for texts that speak to that concern.

Remember that *perceived* needs are not the only ones we address. Let Scripture itself dictate the agenda for your preaching. It is what God wants to say to people that really matters, not what we want to say or hear. Beware of having an idea in search of a text to support it. In the final analysis, the text itself must determine the subject of the sermon. Find out what sort of teaching your prospective listeners have been receiving. If it has mainly been reproof, correction, or training in righteousness, you might consider supplementing that with preaching that includes more doctrinal content.

Don't leave text selection until too late. With so many steps to follow, this should be done well in advance of the preaching opportunity. A great advantage of consecutive exposition of texts from a single Bible book is that this agonizing decision doesn't have to be made so often. We only need to discern how much of the book to expound for each week.

## 2. Read the Text Carefully and Repeatedly
This may seem obvious, but too many preachers neglect it. Jumping into study pushes you toward dissecting the text before you have a feel for it as a whole in its context. So read it prayerfully and thoughtfully several times in the copy of the Bible from which you plan to preach. Then read it in various translations, the more literal the better. Read it aloud. Read it with the emphasis and phrasing

---

[2]Stanley P. Saunders, 'Revelation and Resistance: Narrative and Worship in John's Apocalypse,' in Joel B. Green and Michael Pasquarello III, eds. *Narrative Reading, Narrative Preaching*, 117-150 (Grand Rapids: Baker, 2003).

that help you actually communicate its content and intent as you read. Say what the text is saying using its words. You may *hear* things you did not *see*. As you read, make some notes of things you observe. Ask the Lord to bring your mind into submission to it. Read the immediate literary context of your text, the chapters before and after it. I assume you have recently read the whole book from which the text comes. Doing this again as many times as you can manage will dramatically increase your ability to see in your text what the author is getting at in the book as a whole and what your text adds to those repeated themes. The earlier you start prayerfully reading and rereading your text, the sooner you will be ready to move to step three.

## 3. Study the Text; that is, Engage in Exegesis

For some people, Bible study, whether undertaken alone or in a small group, is an exercise in saying what comes to their minds when they read a passage of Scripture. This sort of free association is not our goal in preparing to preach. We want to discover what the original author is driving at so that we can understand what God might want to say to us through that thought. Bible study is a highly disciplined undertaking in which we submit our thoughts to the writer's thoughts. It is based on the assumption that we can discover what words, phrases, and sentences mean in various syntactical arrangements. What they mean is what we want to know. We may choose to study on our knees as a reminder to ourselves of our submission to God's Word, and we will certainly want to be praying that he will reveal his mind to us, but the answer to our prayers will not be ideas that are at odds with what the words themselves are saying. Spiritual sensitivity is not a substitute for the disciplined work of study but the complement to it. It prepares us to see what is in the text; it does not excuse us from looking hard at the text to discover it.

Some excellent books have been written on how to study the Bible.[3] These are really worth reading and putting their insights into

---

[3]Gordon Fee and Douglas Stuart wrote *How to Read the Bible for All Its Worth,* 2nd ed. (Grand Rapids: Zondervan, 1993) and *How to Read the Bible Book by Book: A Guided Tour* (Grand Rapids: Zondervan, 2002).

practice. We learn to study the Bible mainly by studying it. What follows is a highly condensed recitation of practices that will help you discover what the Lord is saying so you can say it on his behalf. Remember to pray before, during, and after the entire study process.

Find a place to study where you can concentrate and actually think about what you are reading. Learn what distracts you and try to stay clear of it. If you use a computer in the process, don't let it sidetrack you. If you need a clear desk, don't spend all your time clearing it. It may be wiser to go to the library. If the telephone could ring, ask someone else ahead of time to answer it or let an answering machine answer it. Make sure you have the necessary tools at hand.

Discipline yourself not to think too much at this stage about your need for a sermon or even about your listeners' perceived needs. Those concerns can contaminate the study process, keeping you from seeing what is actually in the text. The rush to premature application has spoiled many a sermon.

Make an initial assessment of the genre of the text, that is, determine what sort of literature it is. Is it poetry, narrative, apocalyptic, or something else? This will help you know what features to expect and therefore alert you to things like parallelism in poetry that you wouldn't look for in narrative.[4]

Read the text in the original language if you can. Make your own translation, writing it out in a form that reflects its structure. For example, you may want to write *independent* clauses at the left margin and to indent *dependent* clauses to show their supportive function. Put prepositional phrases under the words they modify. Indent correlative conjunctions at the same level in your outline to give you a visual reminder of their parallel status, and so on. If you do not know the original languages, do the same structural analysis based on a good, modern, literal translation of the Bible.[5] In the

---

[4]See, for instance, Thomas G. Long, *Preaching the Literary Forms of the Bible* (Philadelphia: Fortress, 1989), and Steven D. Mathewson, *The Art of Preaching Old Testament Narrative* (Grand Rapids: Baker, 2002).

[5]The NASB and the ESV would serve this purpose well. *Young's Literal Translation* may be too literal, but can nevertheless help you spot syntactical relationships.

process you will be more or less forced to observe individual words, especially connectives of various kinds. You will observe purpose clauses and result clauses. You will have to distinguish between nouns and verbs. In the latter case, notice tense, number, and other features. Key theological words like grace, hope, love, fear, and truth will repay more detailed study. Repeated words or concepts will be especially significant. You will look for examples of particularization and generalization. Note these carefully, for it is of the essence of preaching to make valid generalizations and apply particulars in the text to specific contemporary situations. You will see causation and substantiation, promise and fulfillment, instrumentation, and contrasts of various sorts. Look for explanations so you can use them to explain the text to your listeners. Summaries and editorial comments are especially useful. Characters, dialogue, and plot are the stuff of narrative passages. Look for images and descriptions that communicate more than the words alone. These are especially common in poetry. The list could go on. The point is to develop habits in study that make you observe and take seriously every part of the passage. Every word is there for a reason. Your task is to discover what that reason is and see how it contributes to the message the text as a whole is designed to convey.

Pay particular attention to the immediate literary context, allowing the surrounding passages to alert you to what is in your text. Check parallel passages or use a concordance to let other biblical texts shed additional light on this one.

This process of study, or your own personalized version of it, will yield a mass of observations from even the shortest text. You will want to write down these thoughts as they occur to you, perhaps alongside your structural outline or in some way that makes them easy to retrieve. If you use a computer for this purpose, you may lose some of the ability to have everything in view at once.

How do you glean valid information from this collection of observations that will help you begin to focus your study toward preaching, toward actually expounding this text? The most useful means I have found is to *interrogate* the text, asking questions of it that force you not only to observe *what* is there but to see *why* it is there.[6] Consider using or adapting the following six questions – as I have adapted them from others. When thoughtfully answered, they will help you be faithful both to the content of the text and its intent, the *what* and *why* of the text.

i) **What is *this text*, functionally?**[7] That is, on the basis of its content and structure, what does it seem designed to do? Is there a name for that? Is it, for instance, a reminder, an explanation, a plea, a rebuke, a command, a description, or something else? Notice that this is not the same thing as asking about the genre of the text. That is a much more general category. This question forces you to look more closely at a smaller unit of text to see what purpose is built into it. There will be clues that help us answer this question. Statements in the imperative mood, for instance, point toward commands or exhortations. The presence of woes or other negative consequences suggests a warning; positive outcomes may signal a promise. Purpose and result clauses alert the reader to an argument, or to an explanation, or to some cause-and-effect relationship. A story may well be an example.[8] Other features may lead us to conclude that the text is a description, a rebuke, or that an event is being reported. The text may be a functional combination, such as an exhortation followed by reasons for obeying it. If we don't ask this question, we may be tempted to turn everything into an exhortation, when simple observation tells us that it is something else altogether.

ii) **What is the main thing *this text* is speaking about?**[9] Answering this question requires weighing the various things the author mentions and discerning which of them is central. Sometimes in narrative, the subject itself is implicit. The story could be an example of loyalty or divine providence without the words themselves

---

[6]This material has previously appeared, among other places, as 'God's Letter of Intent,' *The Art and Craft of Biblical Preaching* (Grand Rapids: Zondervan, 2005).

[7]See Walter L. Liefeld, *New Testament Exposition* (Grand Rapids: Zondervan, 1984), 95-114.

[8]1 Corinthians 10:11 cites an Old Testament story that is both an example and a warning.

[9]Questions 2 and 3 are suggested by Haddon Robinson, *Biblical Preaching*, 41 ff.

being used. Recalling the themes of the Bible book may alert us to their presence in the text at hand. Every passage is about God and about humanity, yet for preaching we must narrow down the answer. A valid answer to this question could be a word, such as *prayer, faith, hope,* or *judgment.* It could be a phrase such as 'God's dealings with the nations'. There are usually several possible answers to this question. For example, if you are studying 1 Peter 3:1-7, possible answers might include

· 'mutual submission at home' (based on the 'likewise', vv. 3, 7, linking this section to earlier teaching about submission and the use of that word in vv. 1, 5);
· 'holiness in marriage' (based on the example in v. 5);
· 'duties of husbands and wives.'

You have to decide which best captures the essence of the whole text. The value of this question is straightforward. If the passage is about prayer, our message from this text should be about prayer. We preach about what the text is speaking about.

iii) **What is *this text* saying about its subject?** If we have accurately discerned the subject of the text, everything else in it will relate to the subject in some discernable and supportive way. The answer to the previous question will be a word or phrase; the answer to this one will be a sentence. To answer this question, we read the text to let it say what it will about the subject. If the subject is prayer, the answer to this third question may be, 'Prayer is essential' or 'Prayer is too-often neglected'. If parts of the passage do not say something about the subject, revisit the second question to see if another answer is better. This summary sentence is what we will later refer to as the *thrust* of the passage.

iv) **What response does *this text* call for?** Accurate answers to the first three questions already incline us to certain answers to this question. So a text that is an *exhortation* concerning the *indispensability of prayer* fairly dictates the response a sermon from this text should seek: *pray!* Nevertheless, we want to let the text call for the response its author has in mind, not the one we think of. Something in the text or context will indicate the sort of response the author is aiming for in writing the text. Conversely, many responses, though worthwhile in themselves, are not what the text you are studying is aiming to elicit. Validity in application begins with an accurate answer to this question. The response may well be a change in attitude, thinking, feeling, or will, as well as some specific action. The text may call for more than one response. The intended response may be implied, but be careful not to read implied exhortations into every passage. To ask and answer this question with integrity is to repent of the textual abuse of commandeering a text as a pretext for a response *we* want as opposed to the one(s) God intends.

v) **How does *this text* elicit that response?** This question helps us *expound* the text as opposed to vaguely referring to it. Here we look more closely at the features of the text, now not for how they develop the subject (question 3) but for how they move the listener toward the response the author intended . When preached as God's word, the Bible goes to work in those who receive it as it is (1 Thess. 2:13). This question looks for ways this text transforms the life of the believer by renewing the mind (Rom. 12:1-2), and how it sanctifies him or her (John 17:17). Does it appeal to the hearer's mind, emotions, will, conscience, sense of duty, love for God, sense of need, or love of the truth? Does it use questions, examples, reminders, word pictures, Scripture citations, or argumentation? Is the means employed repetitive, hitting the same note again and again, or is it more cumulative, building a case for the desired response by a range of rhetorical techniques? Your message may use additional legitimate means of moving people to valid responses, but to neglect those within the passage itself is a mistake that robs the sermon of authority, implying that without our help the message won't come through powerfully enough.

vi) **How does *this text* contribute to the larger drama of redemption?** The previous questions may lead the preacher to thoughts that are consistent with the text but are inadequate because they are out of touch with how this passage fits into the larger picture. Each preaching portion is an integral part of the biblical book in which it is found, but also contributes to the history of redemption, and in some discernable way points to Christ. Our task as Christian preachers is to discover the connections and articulate them. For example, when we preach Psalm 110 we do not speak only, or even mainly, about David, but about Jesus, who applies it to himself, as do Peter and the writer to the Hebrews.[10] We discover that the Father is expressing to the Son his unshakeable commitment to the Son's lordship. Until we preach that, we haven't really done justice to Psalm 110. Of course, other Old Testament passages are not so clearly linked to Christ, but according to Luke 24:27 all of them serve this Christocentric purpose in one way or another.

Careful study of the biblical text is the bedrock of faithful preaching. If you don't have good answers to these questions, the likelihood is that you will just say what comes to mind when you read the text. Effective preaching is not just about saying what we should say from a text; it is also about avoiding saying things we shouldn't or needn't say. Too many messages are wielded as 'blunt instruments' because we include ideas that, while true and helpful, don't really arise from the text. The Bible constrains us to think in certain ways and preach the thoughts it insists upon. Questions like these can help us discover those thoughts as we move from the study of the text to structuring our sermon from it. Before you move forward, one thing remains.

Check your conclusions and observations by the best commentaries you can secure. These will confirm or challenge your thinking and will introduce fruitful ideas that you hadn't considered. Biblical scholars publish very helpful lists of the most useful commentaries.[11] If you are not in a position to buy them, check them out of the library, use interlibrary loan if your local library doesn't own them, or borrow them from other pastors or laypeople. Other sources of good older commentaries include garage sales, used book sales, secondhand bookstores, thrift stores and web sites that include used books. Sometimes people want to give gifts to their pastor, but don't know what to give. Having a wish-list of commentaries

---

[10]Matthew 22:41-45; Acts 2:34-36; Hebrews 1:13; 5:6; 7:17, 21.

[11]For example, D.A. Carson, *New Testament Commentary Survey* (Grand Rapids: Baker Academic, 2007).

for such occasions blesses both giver and receiver. Read introductions to commentaries to get the lay of the land. Read more technical commentaries before reading the popular ones. Read older commentaries sparingly since the best insights from them will usually be quoted in newer works, but don't assume that newer is always better. Don't use commentaries as a short-cut to developing a sermon, or to quote in a message. Use them to help you spot themes, understand the context, clarify difficult passages, and for pointers in integrating your text with the rest of the book. Systematic theologies and other introductions to the Bible that have good Scripture indexes can be a great help in seeing how your text fits into the larger pattern of Biblical truth. Although this is the last part of *studying* the text, planning well ahead will make sure you have the books available when you need them.

## 4. Meditate on the Text, Humbly Inviting God to Speak to You Through It that You Might Obey It.

Ideally, your study of the text will thrill your heart with its life-giving truths and move you to respond to it. Your study will stretch your mind, feed your soul, and thrill your heart as you rejoice in what you learn about God and his ways and your need for his grace individually and as a church. You will be filled with gratitude and genuinely want to respond with faith and obedience. In practice, when faced with deadlines, pressures and other responsibilities, we are easily tempted to press on with crafting the sermon even when the text has not penetrated our hearts. We may think of all the things yet to do before Sunday and conclude that we just don't have time to meditate on the text, pondering its meaning, and reflecting on our lives in light of its teaching. In reality, we cannot afford *not* to do so. It is not just that the message will not ring true with our listeners if we preach, as my friend Don Loomer puts it, 'from the teeth out'. That is bad enough, but it is not the worst consequence. The greater problem is what happens to our own souls when we treat revelation from God as a commodity in which we trade, a mere resource for our sermons, something we serve up to others without actually feeding upon it ourselves. Inevitably a hardening sets in, that renders us progressively unable to hear God's truths. When we fail to take the Bible seriously we are not merely hypocrites, we sink to the level of mere peddlers of God's word (2 Cor. 2:17). Few things devalue a message more than a messenger who proves by disregarding it that he doesn't really believe it.

So what are we to do? Remember who you are in the sight of God. Although you are his messenger, you are also a needy recipient. You need the word of life as much as anyone to whom you will speak. You and I must be grateful listeners before we can be faithful speakers. Start the preparation process early so you have time to undertake each step in the process thoughtfully, and devotionally. Feeding on Scripture simply cannot be rushed. Build into your life times and places to ponder, consider, and ruminate. Expect this to be difficult in an activist society, but anticipate that your practice will improve with time. God will honor your desire to submit to his word. Use a journal or notepad to focus your thoughts. Invite the Holy Spirit to search your heart, using the word as his scalpel (Heb. 4:12-13). Focus your application of the text, based on your answer to question 4 in the previous chapter. If God is already making progress in your life in the ways called for by the text, celebrate that and thank him. Think of at least one specific, sustainable step of obedience God wants you to take, and invite support from others to take it. Ask God to help you develop habits that become part of who you are as he uses his word to reshape and sanctify you. Don't try to do too much. Remember that a valid response may well be worship, repenting of unworthy thoughts, or inviting God to inculcate an attitude as well as specific actions such as seeking reconciliation.

If you discover that your attempts truly to hear and heed God's word fail, don't give up. Wait upon the Lord until he speaks to you and turns you toward him. Forging ahead without knowing his mind can be disastrous, as Saul found out to his peril. When Samuel failed to meet Saul's deadline, the king pressed ahead and offered an unauthorized sacrifice. That disobedience cost Saul his throne (1 Sam. 13:7-14). Look for something in your life that might be amiss, a sin that requires confession and repentance, a relationship that needs healing, an idol that needs smashing, or a priority that needs re-ordering. Ask God if you have missed the real point of the text. Perhaps the word is not going to work in you because you have unwittingly twisted it. When we sincerely ask God to show us why we cannot hear his voice, he will tell us so that we may respond in faith and obedience.

When you let the word wash *you* (Eph. 5:26), the sense of reality will come through in your preaching. The message will not only come from God but from your own heart. People will know it instinctively. The old, old story will be fresh and vital because it is good news for you on the day you deliver it.

# 14

# Letting the Text Have Its Say

## 5. Summarize the Thrust of the Text in a Single Sentence

By the *thrust of the text* I mean the heart of its message – the answer
to the question, 'What is this text saying about what it is talking
about?'[1] We don't ask what this has to do with our listeners until the
next step, because to lump the two together too often lets us rush to
application before we can state the truth of the text we are applying.

Consider an example. Let's say you select as your text
Jeremiah 5:1-31. If you study it carefully and focus your study
by asking the six questions suggested above, you might answer
the first three as follows. Functionally, this text is part of an oracle
(4:27). God is speaking, lamenting the rebellion of his people.
God is instructing Jeremiah to declare a specific message. We
judge the *subject* to be God's impending judgment on his
rebellious people. What is this text saying about that subject?
God says that this judgment is justified, imminent, and will be
devastatingly thorough, but also gracious. Even before we
proceed to answer the last three questions (concerning the
response sought, how it is elicited, and how this text fits into the
larger drama of redemption), we already know the thrust of the
passage: *God is fully justified in judging his willfully rebellious
subjects but does not make full use of his right to do so.* We
know this is what the text is getting at even before we ask what
it has to do with our immediate listeners. That means we know
what we are going to speak about when we preach – *God's
justice in judging sin* – and what we are going to say about it –
*God is justified in judging, but merciful.* This provides the
foundation for exhortation. Until we have made the case from

---

[1] Ramesh Richard, *Preparing Expository Sermons* (Grand Rapids: Baker,
2001), 66, calls this 'the heart of the passage, the central proposition of the
text'. I prefer the word *thrust* and confine the word 'proposition' to a part of
the *sermon*.

the text that this passage faithfully describes the unchanging God and clearly articulate what we learn about him, we are not ready to challenge anyone to do anything. Imperatives *follow* indicatives. If we skip this step we will build our sermons on flimsy foundations.

Why do we summarize the thrust of the text in a single sentence? We do so because if two sentences are necessary then we probably should preach two sermons from this text. Every preaching portion has multiple thoughts, but they should all point in one direction and have a single thrust – what the author wants us to grasp and respond to. That is what we summarize in a single simple sentence with no semicolons allowed. A biblical sermon is not a loose collection of concepts all found in a text of Scripture. *It is a clear restatement of the dominant truth of the text* (its thrust) *preached for the purpose for which it was given.* All the other thoughts in the text exist to develop the thrust or to help listeners respond rightly to it.

You may legitimately ask, 'May I preach a biblically faithful sermon whose main claim, what we will presently label the proposition, is *not* built upon the main thrust of the text?' After all, you might argue, one could preach a rich, accurate message on Christology from Philippians 2:5-11 even though in its context that text is part of an exhortation, an encouragement to like-mindedness rooted in the humility of which Christ is the supreme example. Would that be legitimate? Remember that *preaching is not just teaching* – it contains teaching, but it always aims for a response. Certainly, a faithful preacher could focus on verses 6-11 and invite listeners to respond by submission and worship, marveling in God's grace and Christ's obedience in the incarnation. Eventually, however, one would want to harness the text's glorious Christology to the purpose for which the writer included it in the text – an example of the humility that makes community possible. Worship of Christ is an *implied* response that should not be neglected. But it is wiser for the beginner to look for the *explicit* purpose of the text and preach it for that purpose before seeking secondary, though valid, applications.

To take another example, may we preach a textually faithful sermon on how to listen to Christian preaching from Acts 10:33b? *('Now we are all here in the presence of God to listen to everything the Lord has commanded you to tell us.')* This could be legitimate if the handling of the Old Testament by writers of the New is allowed to inform our answer. We may cite and employ a text to *illustrate* a biblical truth that is not manifestly the thrust of that text when the truth itself is plainly taught in other passages of Scripture and the text we are employing is, at a minimum, reminiscent of that biblical truth. Thus, in Acts 10, we know that God is *present* when people are gathered in his name to hear his word expounded and that he has *commanded the preacher* to tell the listeners what his word teaches. Further, we know that we are not to listen selectively, but to *everything* the preacher legitimately preaches from Scripture. Cornelius mentions these ideas in his invitation to Peter. We should heed Cornelius' *implicit* advice to listen reverently, attentively, and expectantly. The text supplies a narrative framework from the context in Acts from which to communicate the thought. However, if we employ the text this way (and I have done so), I think we owe it to our listeners to state clearly what the thrust of the passage is and that we are, in this sermon, underscoring a secondary, even peripheral thought, but one that is faithful to the whole of scriptural teaching. When the preacher expounds books of the Bible taking each section sequentially, an occasional excursus that picks up a minor thought can enrich rather than undermine the whole series.

That exception notwithstanding, the main idea stands. Until you can write this single sentence articulating the thrust of the passage, you are not ready to proceed. If you do, you may find yourself merely reporting what strikes your fancy or, worse, what you think your listeners will like. Our goal is to give voice to what *God* is saying so that our listeners will respond *to him*. Until we can articulate what he is saying, we aren't ready to describe the response we (and the text) seek.

## 6. Discern how this Text Speaks to Your Listeners. Write out a provisional proposition, that is, the thrust of the passage as it relates to your listeners.

So far, in preparing the message we have focused on the text of Scripture and have deliberately postponed considering the specific needs of our hearers, lest we read into the text solutions to those needs. Now, having determined what we believe to be the thrust of the passage, we lift our eyes from the text and take a hard look at the congregation we expect to address. We ask the Lord to show us what the text's thrust has to do with the people to whom we will speak. In our choice of a text we have already thought of our listeners' needs and circumstances in a general way. In our study of the text we have asked what response it seems designed to elicit. Now, we build into the proposition a response that reflects this. So, for instance, if an Old Testament text describes the sin of idolatry and calls for repentance, we will preach for repentance from idolatry but will remind our listeners, as the New Testament does, that idolatry is more than bowing down to graven images (Col. 3:5).

It helps to recall the range of possible human needs. The Bible portrays marred people, distorted by the fall. Human twistedness appears in various shapes. Some needs are universal. Everyone since Adam needs to experience conviction of sin. Everyone needs to be reminded that we were made to worship God. We all need wisdom, knowledge, encouragement, hope, and reminders of God's righteousness and grace, to name a few. There are also needs you perceive in the congregation, outcroppings of fallenness that you as a preacher should address. These might include the need for more maturity, greater unity, or more patience. Then there are the expressed needs of the congregation, matters they ask you to address from Scripture. These may include doctrinal questions, lifestyle concerns, spiritual disciplines, specific guidance, or some other down-to-earth matter. You will recall that the congregation is made up of individuals whose needs vary. Your responsibility is to tailor what the text calls for to your contemporary listeners. You don't dilute its demands but you do contextualize them, transposing the melody line of the text into a key your listeners can sing. You have already thought of the response called for by the text. Now that you are alert to the range of needs represented in your listeners, you express within the proposition the specific response sought by the text that corresponds to the actual needs of your listeners.

The proposition is *the thrust of the text as it relates to the listeners*. Both phrases in the definition of the proposition are crucial. *The thrust of the text* must be stated, if only in a very condensed fashion. This is the truth, the reality that mandates the intended response. It must be there. But a proposition is not merely the statement of a theological or spiritual truth, however glorious or foundational. In addition to that truth, the proposition states, either explicitly or implicitly, *what that truth has to do with one's listeners*. Without this component a sermon is merely an exercise in conveying Bible knowledge. God wants to be heard. But he does not mean for us to acknowledge merely that a message has reached our ears. We haven't really *heard* God until we obey him. In some biblical texts, hearing and obeying are virtually synonymous.[2] We haven't rightly crafted a sermon if we neglect to wed the truth and the required response into a single, forceful sentence.

I have called this sentence a *provisional* proposition because when we begin to develop this proposition in the outline of the sermon, we may discover that it needs to be revised to fit the data the text supplies. But provisional or not, it must be written, and this is both the hardest and most important task in sermon construction. What makes it so *important* is that it is the verbal bridge between the text and the congregation. If we get it right it will faithfully summarize how this text is inviting them to respond to God. Everything that follows in the sermon is there because the proposition calls for it. Everything we decide to leave out, we omit because the proposition makes it unnecessary.

What makes the proposition so *difficult* to write are the high standards we will have for this sentence. Since it summarizes our message and is the one thing we want people to take home with them, it should be *memorable,* although never catchy at the expense of accuracy. Indeed, it needs to be memorable enough that *we* can

---

[2] G. A. Lee, 'Hear; Hearken; Listen; Obey, etc.' *International Standard Bible Encyclopedia* (Grand Rapids: Eerdmans, 1982), 2:649.

remember it and urge it upon people repeatedly without reference to notes. It must be *clear*. Clarity is aided by *conciseness*, using as few words as will get the job done. This is not brevity at the expense of adequacy. It should be *comprehensive,* but not wordy. The proposition does not say everything we will say in the sermon, but it does accurately summarize the whole thing. It is not a past-tense statement about what Jeremiah or Peter did in their days, but about what we are to be and do today. It is *contemporary* and its wording reflects that. Above all, a thoughtful listener, filled with the Holy Spirit, would agree that this statement accurately calls for the response God wants based on the truth this passage teaches.

A proposition that achieves these lofty but important goals will seldom emerge on your first attempt to write it. You will need to write and rewrite, edit and edit again. The proposition is like the DNA of your sermon. If you state clearly for your listeners what this passage is saying to them and how they should respond, the balance of your message is just a matter of developing that idea in an orderly fashion patterned after how the text does that and driving it home in ways the text suggests. If you miss the mark here, you will constantly struggle to coerce the text to say and do what you have wrongly declared that it says and does.

Let us consider an example. If we decide that Malachi 2:1-9 is a valid preaching portion, study it in detail and interrogate it, we readily discover that this text is an *admonition*, a word used in the text itself to describe what it is (vv. 1, 4, NIV). Next, noticing the words in verse 7, we conclude that this text is about 'the messenger of the LORD Almighty'. This is its subject. In Malachi's day, those who fulfilled this role were Levitical priests. What is this text saying about such messengers? God is against those messengers who forsake the foundational requirements of this office. What is the intended response? God seeks repentance from the messengers so that true instruction would be restored, knowledge would be preserved, people would no longer be caused to stumble, his covenant with Levi would continue, and ultimately his name would be honored. How does God, speaking through Malachi, seek to elicit this response? The text notes the ideal (vv. 4-7), the reality which falls far short of that ideal (vv. 2, 8, 9), and God's vigorous response to the unacceptable difference (vv. 2, 3, 9).

If these observations are accurate, then the *thrust* of the passage might be stated, 'God is against his messengers who do not listen to him, honor him, or speak rightly for him.' That is a true and accurate statement that reflects what the passage is getting at. However, it is not yet a *proposition* because it does not tell us *what that truth has to do with us as listeners*. We turn it into a proposition by stating what that truth means for us who read this passage and hear it preached today. Such a proposition might be, 'If you despise your calling as God's messenger, don't expect God to sit idly by.' That sentence encapsulates the thrust of the passage, but expresses it in a way calculated to achieve the purpose for which the text was given, namely, repentance. Since repentance is fundamentally a change of mind, the proposition urges us as preachers to think seriously about God's attitude toward those who, by turning from the way, culpably fail to honor his name (v. 8), and to soberly consider the consequences of such irresponsibility. If you were preaching this passage to a congregation who were almost entirely nonpreachers you might word the proposition differently, such as, 'Take your pastor's calling as seriously as God does.' The essential content of the sermon would be the same, but it would take into account the different *situation* of most of its hearers.

In each of these examples, both necessary parts of the proposition are present in content, although not separate in form. Some recommend a more standardized form of proposition that does separate the two and sounds like this: 'Because ... *(biblical truth)*, we should ... *(response sought)*.' Using a set form has value, especially for beginners, but it can blunt the force of the thought, and can begin to sound too predictable if you are preaching to the same people every week. The important thing is that both truth and response are there, whether stated or implied. You may choose to use more of the language of the text itself in the proposition, but I don't think that is necessary as long as the development of the proposition is thoroughly biblical in language, content, and form.

If the proposition does not become clear to you by deriving it from the thrust of the passage, attack it from the other angle. Look at the individual elements in the passage, truths that you can confidently anchor to specific verses. Lay these out and try to discern what they add up to. That is the thrust of the passage. Then try to discover why they are there. That is the response that you will build in to the proposition.

For instance, in Titus 1:1-3 the apostle Paul is speaking about his ministry. He is saying several things about that ministry that may not immediately seem to fit into a clear pattern. But once we lay them out, the pattern emerges. We notice that his ministry is *rooted in the character of God* of whom Paul is a servant. (God does not lie, promises eternal life, brings his word to light through preaching.) Second, we observe that Paul's ministry is *obedient to the call of God* who commanded him to preach, entrusting the message to him. We see next that Paul's ministry is *faithful to the word of God* because it rests squarely on the hope that God's word brings. Finally, we realize that Paul's ministry is *for the people of God*, or as the text puts it, 'for the faith of God's elect.' When we get all these pieces of the puzzle on the table we see the connection. At the heart of ministry is God himself whose character, call, word, and people supply the foundation, direction, content, and object of our ministries. The *thrust* of the passage might be, 'God is at the heart of valid ministry.' Since *every* believer has a ministry, your proposition might be, 'Let God have his rightful place in your ministry.' The truth imbedded here is that God does have a central place in ministry. The response sought is self-examination and correction of our view and practice of ministry by the insights of this text. The next steps will explain and demonstrate how we develop the proposition.

# 15

# Working to Make the Message Clear

**7. Structure your Message in a Way that Reflects how the Text is Designed to Achieve its God-given Purposes. Describe how your message will develop the proposition by means of an organizational sentence.**
You know from your study of the text what it is functionally, what it is saying about a subject, and what response it seeks. You also have some thoughts about how it seeks to elicit that response. You have drafted a proposition that expresses how the thrust of the passage relates to your listeners. Now you need to develop that seminal thought in a way that reflects how the passage develops it and will make sense to your listeners. The crucial step to which we now come is simply telling your listeners what you are going to do. You owe it to your hearers to let them in on how your message is going to make its case for what you propose. This is done by the *organizational sentence*. The organizational sentence is defined as that element of the sermon that describes how the main points of the sermon will develop the proposition. The organizational sentence helps *you*, because it puts you on record that the sermon *will* develop the proposition according to a clear plan. It helps *the listeners* by providing confidence that this message is going somewhere and that you the speaker know the destination. It gives the listener pegs on which to hang the thoughts to come – specific auditory sign-posts for which to listen. What follows will not meander or ramble; it will be logical and purposeful. The best organizational sentences say very little about the content of the message – that is the job of the proposition and the outline. The organizational sentence restricts itself to alerting the listener to how the sermon organizes this content.

Consider the following four types of organizational sentences, with some examples and attendant weaknesses of each.

The **general** organizational sentence would be something like, 'My remarks today come in two parts, investigation and application,' or 'To profit from this message we need to hear first, what the apostle Paul is saying to the Ephesians, and second, what God wants to say through him to us.' Both of these are significantly better than nothing. They alert the listener to a two-point message, the first part being a look at the text, and the second a derived application. They fulfill the purpose of the organizational sentence, but they don't tell us anything about how either part of the message will be developed.

The **key word** organizational sentence championed by my late homiletics professor, Dr. Lloyd Perry, and used by his students around the world, is easy to understand and use. It employs a key word in the plural, modified by a number that corresponds to the number of main points in the outline that follows, plus sufficient verbiage to explain how the items so labeled (by the key word) will develop the proposition. For example, 'The apostle Paul supplies *three reasons* to obey this command,' or 'As we study this passage, we will discover *four truths* about Christ's death.' Listeners who are paying any attention at all now know to listen for the three reasons or four truths. The outline supplies them and the message achieves significant clarity. This sort of outline is admirably memorable and picks up parallels between parts of the passage that the casual reader of the text may not have noticed.

The greatest danger of the key word organizational sentence is that it may tempt us to squeeze the passage into a mold, seeing similarities or parallels that are not actually there. A second weakness is that we may use a key word that is too general: 'We are going to learn three things today.' A third danger is using a key word that is inaccurate. For instance, it is misleading to say 'Peter gives us four commands to obey' when actually he supplies two truths and two commands. A fourth pitfall, especially for the novice, is thinking that the key word is the same thing as the subject of the passage. It is not. It only describes what the main points of the outline have in common. A fifth danger is fixating on the relationship between the main points to the neglect of the more important relationship between the outline as a whole and the proposition the main points develop.

Despite these dangers, the key word organizational sentence is a handy tool when used carefully.

The **rhetorically driven** organizational sentence looks carefully at the text itself and describes its parts in ways that help the listeners follow the argument of the text itself, and therefore of the sermon being preached from it. For instance, you might say, 'This story is like a book with four chapters.' Then you say, 'Chapter 1,' and begin telling the first of four parts of the story, applying it piecemeal or as a whole depending upon what the text calls for. Or, you might say, 'Paul's argument has a premise, a conclusion, and an application.' The listeners know that the message to be preached will have three parts, but instead of being invited to listen for three 'parts' (a word that emphasizes what they have in common), he or she now knows to listen for three different elements that are organic to the text itself and add up to an argument or make a case.

You might be obliged to say, 'Here the writer to the Hebrews issues a warning followed by two consequences of disobedience and one blessing of obedience.' Now the listener knows that the message will have four parts – one warning, two consequences and one blessing, yet his or her focus is not on the total number of elements in the outline but on how they develop the author's thought.

The great strength of this type of organizational sentence is that it grounds the whole exposition in the text itself. Many sermons that start out promising a biblically grounded message stray from that good intention when the preacher's organizational preferences mask the original author's inspired rhetoric. The closer the message is to the rhetorical strategy of the text the better. It must be said, however, that sometimes this type of organizational sentence is cumbersome and strikes fear in the heart of the listener that what is coming is a lecture instead of a sermon. If the rhetorical strategy of the text is complicated, it may be better to develop a sermon plan that is simple and consider how the text makes its point later as you develop the outline itself. In such a case you might say, 'Our text today addresses three crucial questions.' Then show in your outline how the content of the sermon answers those questions. This keeps the organization simpler, while taking time to grapple with the argument itself under each of the three questions addressed in the text.

The **billboard** organizational sentence combines the organizational sentence with a succinct preview of the outline. This type takes its name from the highway advertising sign that must make its point clearly and briefly. The billboard organizational sentence usually limits itself to a word or short phrase for each main point of the outline. 'God wants us to understand the atonement. Our text today will explain its *roots*, its *branches*, and its *fruit*,' or 'To understand salvation, we must grasp its tenses: past, present and future.' Notice that these billboards say very little about the actual content that the outline will develop, but they do provide descriptive hooks on which the listeners can hang the thoughts shortly to be offered. If you say too much about any one of these items, listeners will start taking notes about that point before you are ready to develop it.

However you do it, tell your listeners what to listen for. Don't tell them so much that they will mistake this for the substance of what you will shortly say, but tell the congregation enough that they can see where you are going and are motivated to travel with you. *Don't* tell them what you are going to tell them. That leaves them with no reason to listen. They will already know what you are going to say. *Do* tell them what to listen for. There is a big difference. Remember, the text is your friend in preaching. It is living and active. It wants to be heard. It not only tells you what to say but will point you in the direction of how to say it so that your listeners can take it in.

## 8. Write an Outline that Fulfills the Promises implied by the Proposition and the Organizational Sentence.

The very idea of a sermon outline is not universally accepted. David Buttrick prefers what he calls 'moves', arguing that to number the parts of a sermon is to invite listeners to stop listening.[1] But whatever we call them, the thoughts that develop the central claim of our sermon, the proposition, have to come in some order and we might as well think about that order. Remember, I am not now describing how you announce that you have arrived at the next point, move, or

---

[1] David Buttrick, *Homiletic* (Philadelphia: Fortress, 1987), 69-70.

'main' in your outline; I am only saying that all thought is sequential.[2] Therefore, it makes sense to think about your thoughts and put them in the best order to achieve the text's purposes. Your cultural heritage may lead you to tell stories from a distinctive perspective or to give an account by circling the end-point for a long time before you land. Whatever your cultural conventions, there is a reason why one thought follows another. Outlining is a way of being clear about what we are doing. It reminds us to include only those thoughts that achieve the purposes we have declared in the proposition in ways signaled by the organizational sentence.

Note also that an outline can precede the proposition if we intend to develop the proposition *inductively*. In that case, we start with the biblical material and postpone revealing what it adds up to until we have amassed all the data. When we preach inductively we will still want to alert our listeners to this approach by a simple organizational sentence such as, 'Listen to what Jesus says about the pearl of great price.' Then we offer specific *insights* whether we label them as such or not. These insights form our sermon outline. We conclude by articulating what these insights add up to (the thrust) as it relates to our hearers (the proposition). Inductive preaching is a very effective way of communicating that builds a certain amount of suspense and anticipation into the sermon, but the different order of these three elements – proposition, organizational sentence, and outline – does not free us from arranging the meat of the message in some meaningful way. That is what the outline does. When the sermon is *deductive*, we state the proposition first, followed by the organizational sentence, and then the outline. Some sermons are structured to include both inductive and deductive elements, making the proposition plain early on, but building in suspense about how each part of the text builds toward the proposition. But whether your sermon is inductive, deductive, or some combination of the two, you must show how every part of what you are saying builds toward or flows from the proposition.

Haddon Robinson reminds us that the outline helps us *as preachers*, clarifying how the parts fit together into one unified whole

---

[2] Buttrick, *Homiletic*, 24.

and making it obvious where supportive material is needed. It helps *listeners* by crystallizing the order of the ideas so they can be received in the right sequence.[3] More important than these valuable benefits for clarity of thought is the built-in check on faithfulness. If we require of ourselves that each main point in our outline be clearly anchored to one or more verses in our text, we will know immediately when we have not achieved this. If we cannot follow each main point with a Scripture reference, we know that our outline must be adjusted until we can do so.

As the primary steps you take to urge truth upon your listeners, and to move them toward the faith and obedience it seeks, the main points of your outline must meet certain criteria. Each main must be

- *Accurate*, reflecting what the text calls for. Any inclination to aim for alliteration or any other form of rhetorical cleverness, if used at all, should be resisted until you are sure each sentence reflects what the text is actually saying.

- *Simple*, not complex. Each main should accomplish its own singular purpose. Better to have another point or two than one that tries to cover too much ground.

- *Prescriptive*, as opposed to merely descriptive. It need not be an imperative, but it is directed toward the listener, not a plain recitation of history or fact.

- *Subordinate* to the proposition. Each main develops the proposition in some clear way and is not confused with it. A main point does not restate the thrust of the passage; it develops it. I once heard a student's sermon that challenged listeners in the proposition to *seek* God; and in the outline to *pursue* God. These two words invite essentially the same response. The outline should have told us how or why to seek God.

- *Unique*. Each main should also be tested against every other main point so that they do not duplicate or overlap with each other. 'We should believe in God' is too similar to saying, 'We should trust God.'

---

[3] Haddon Robinson, *Biblical Preaching*, 132.

- *Progressive, usually.* Not always, but often, main points of an outline will indicate movement, gathering momentum. Rarely will they be interchangeable in order. Sometimes the order just reflects that of the passage, and no rhetorical strategy behind that textual order is evident. More often there is a reason for the textual order upon which we will want to capitalize in our sermon outline.

- *A grammatically complete sentence.* It may *answer* a question that we use to introduce it, but each main point will tell us something, not ask us something. Part of the sentence may be repeated to place emphasis on how the mains differ without being guilty of overlap. To return to the example cited earlier from Titus 1:1-3, we might propose, 'You can have a solid ministry.' Then we might alert our listeners in an organizational sentence to *four anchors* to God himself that give ministry stability.

A solid ministry is . . .
1) *rooted* in the character of God (v. 2).
2) *obedient* to the call of God (v. 3).
3) *faithful* to the Word of God vv. (2-3).
4) *for* the people of God (v. 1).

Sometimes, main points will be somewhat symmetrical, having a similar relationship to the proposition. These lend themselves to a key word type of organizational sentence. If the text supplies two or three reasons, consequences, dangers, insights, and these cover the scope of the passage, that is a good way to organize and outline the message.

The points of the outline should add up to the whole message as captured in the proposition. There should be no biblical data left over like an embarrassing extra washer or nut after some mechanical device has been reassembled. Conversely, the outline should not go beyond what stands written, including major insights that the passage does not mention.

How many points should there be in an outline? Let the text tell you. The text itself will shape your sermon. Does that mean that when you preach Galatians 5:22 on the fruit of the Spirit you will have a nine-point outline, one corresponding to each aspect of the fruit? You may be wiser to clump the fruit into related clusters, or to preach several messages developing each part of the fruit in more detail by careful study of other passages that explain or exemplify each virtuous manifestation of the fruit of the Spirit. On the other hand, you may find it wiser to take the paragraph in its context and show how the fruit of the Spirit contrasts with the works of the flesh, and how that contrast helps us understand and live in Christian freedom. Too many points push us in the direction of shallowness in the treatment of each. Moreover, announcing six or eight parts to the sermon in your organizational sentence can send a wave of terror across the congregation, who may take it as a life sentence in the pew.

Remember, the proposition, organizational sentence, and outline fit together logically. The proposition tells the listener what he or she can expect you to say biblically and what that has to do with life. The organizational sentence reveals how you plan to develop that applicable truth. The outline actually does the developing. Sometimes preachers get caught up in one or the other of these three and lose sight of the others; consequently, the three do not match. This frustrates alert listeners who feel the preacher does not know what he is talking about (if the proposition is defective), does not have a clear plan (if the organizational sentence is missing or does not fit) or has not delivered on a promise (if the outline does not do what the first two elements promised). Thus, it is crucial to check the correspondence of these three elements at various stages in preparation and adjust them as necessary. The controlling reality is always the thrust of the passage, closely followed in importance by the way the passage develops that thrust. As we submit to them, our messages will conform more nearly to what God has in mind for our listeners.

# 16

# Preaching Through to the Heart

**9. Develop each Thought in the Outline by Anchoring it to part of the Text, Validating the Connection, Explaining it, Illustrating it, and Applying it.**

This is the substance of the sermon. Here is where you actually serve the meat of the word. This is where you let God's voice be heard. Up to now you have been setting the table, letting the guests see the menu, and providing the appetizers. Here comes the feast. Under each main point in the outline are five undertakings. The first three (anchoring, validating, and explaining), when done well, mark your sermon as a genuine exposition of a passage of Scripture. All five of these undertakings are the way you speak the truth plainly (2 Cor. 4:2), and they should not be set out separately as you preach. They are what you must do to get the message into listeners' hearts and minds. So don't think of these as subpoints to be numbered as part of an outline or separate topics to be addressed. They are ways of driving home the text's parts that add up to its thrust.

*Anchoring* is the simple yet vital task of noting the part of your text from which the point just stated comes. As you write your outline, put verse numbers in parentheses after the simple sentence that constitutes the main point. As you deliver the message you will not only state the main point, and refer to the verse or verses from which you derive it, you will usually read those verses from the text. Each point in the outline must be anchored, and altogether the verse number anchors should account for the whole text.

*Validating* consists of demonstrating that the point you just articulated does indeed arise from the verses you just cited and read. Sometimes this step can be skipped because the statement of the main point is self-evidently what the verse is teaching. Normally, however, you will want explicitly to forge the connection between the point and the verse or verses.

*Explaining* means elaborating the truth that is validly taught in the verses cited so that your hearers can understand it. This is where real teaching takes place. This involves such things as defining terms, restating the truth in other ways, narrowing the concept by saying what it does *not* include, putting the text's thought in its theological context, and using word pictures, analogies, or images that clarify meaning. You may point out verbal connections, cause and effect relationships, result clauses, or other features of the passage that you did not mention when validating the point but that help listeners understand what the writer is driving at. You may, for instance, explain why lists of sins and virtues occur in contexts where the author has just denounced legalism, helping your listeners see how such lists function in the text (Col. 2:20–3:17). Address unspoken concerns of the thoughtful listener. Put yourself in his or her shoes, and answer the questions that the text raises. Explain the nature of the writer's argument. Is it a how-much-more argument like the one Paul uses in Romans 5:1-10? Are there Old Testament texts that the New Testament writer assumes his readers knew and would think of? Is this instance one of a series of events that only really makes sense when we consider all of them together? What does God appear to be doing in this text? How are the persons of the Trinity in evidence in this passage? The sorts of things you say in order to explain a passage are many, limited only by your knowledge of the rest of Scripture and your ability to see how this text drives home its point. The beginning preacher often asks, 'What can I say?' The slightly more experienced preacher asks, 'How can I say all that I should?' The mature preacher asks, 'How can I let God say what he wants to say from this text?' Often, saying less is better than saying more, but we need to say the right things. As you make notes on your sermon outline, learn to jot down all sorts of things that come to mind. Edit these to include only those thoughts that do the best job of making the meaning of the text clear to the widest range of your listeners.

*Illustrating*, as the word implies, means to shed light on something. Illustrations bridge the gap between explanation and application. Some make the thought clearer; others help us picture ourselves obeying it; but all good illustrations move us toward the intended response. Illustrations make truth concrete and personal by giving a 'for instance.' They help us get from the specifics of the original hearers or readers of the text to the particulars of our contemporary situation. They help us *see* in our mind's eye what we have only been *hearing* about so far.[1] We have to do this with words.[2] Good illustrations give us time to digest the truth of Scripture we have been chewing on. They make listening pleasurable and appeal to our wills in ways that make us less defensive. The most important step in illustrating is to be very clear about what you are seeking to illustrate.[3] Think of a situation that is truly analogous, that genuinely parallels the point of the text. Then paint a word picture that makes the point; tell a story that encourages the response; cite a passage that reinforces the teaching; read a quote that lends external authority to your case. Make the link between the illustration and the text clear and explicit. Don't force an illustration that does not quite fit or use a story or other illustration that itself needs to be explained or raises issues instead of solving them. Make sure the illustrations don't dominate the sermon. Make sure the illustrations you use are your own (or are accurately attributed to someone else), that they are factually accurate, and that they don't all reflect a narrow band of interests. If you consult illustration sources, don't use them to get illustrations, but only to learn how good preachers use illustrations so you can devise your own. Make it your goal to avoid illustrations you have heard in other sermons;

---

[1] Richard Collier says of William Booth's preaching, 'But all Booth's meetings, in a sense, were children's meetings; he knew that people like to learn by picture, not by precept.' Richard Collier, *The General Next to God*, 242. It seems to me that the key is to use a judicious combination of precept and picture.

[2] Galatians 3:1 in the NIV says, 'Before your very eyes Jesus Christ was clearly portrayed as crucified.' Paul drew a picture, as it were, with his words of public proclamation.

[3] Jack Hughes, *Expository Preaching with Word Pictures with Illustrations from the Sermons of Thomas Watson*, Ross-shire, U.K.: Mentor/ Christian Focus Publications, 2001.

you may be sure that if you have heard them in a sermon, some of your listeners have too. Instead, ask the Lord to show you what would make the thought of the passage clear and would move your listeners to respond appropriately. Devise your own fresh illustrations using your God-given creativity. Reading widely will supply the raw material for illustrations, sometimes providing the perfect quotation or contemporary instance of the problem the text of Scripture addresses. More often, it will help you describe the perennial human predicament in contemporary language.

*Applying* is the general word for helping your listeners respond in the mind, heart, and will to the text in ways for which the text itself calls. Application is built into the very fabric of the sermon since the proposition includes it. We brought focus to our *study* of the text by interrogating it, including questions that unearth the functional shape of the passage, why the Holy Spirit put this text into the Bible, and what response it seems to call for. It is important to keep in mind the answer to that last issue and how the text seems to elicit the called-for response. Although application is everywhere in the sermon, it does not follow that we try to apply every thought we articulate. Some of the thoughts build toward a final truth that alone is the one to be applied. To make our listeners do something in response to some parts of a passage may do an injustice to the role of that part in the text. As always, the text itself determines when and how we seek response. The immediate context will always point you toward a valid application of your text because each text functions in a context to achieve the purpose of the whole. If you are stumped concerning what response to call for, read around your text again, asking how your text contributes to the overall goal of that section of Scripture. Remember, response may not necessarily be mainly or exclusively action. It may be addressed to the whole congregation as well as individuals within it. It may address a sin of omission as well as sins of commission.

Invite people to respond with whatever the text calls for, suggesting specific ways the obedience of faith will manifest itself. You won't be able to state a specific response that precisely fits every listener, but the fact that you have a few specifics will help all your listeners realize that this message is meant to be obeyed.[4] They will be able to extrapolate from the specifics they have heard to the specifics the Holy Spirit will bring to mind for them. Remember to apply the text through the lens of grace and with the motive of love. That is the way the Word of God came to you and it is the way you are to communicate it to others. Make sure your tone fits the tone of the text. Let the cross shape your pleas for response, calling for gospel obedience made possible by the indwelling Holy Spirit. Teach with all patience, recognizing that all spiritual problems are by nature recurrent and all solutions are partial this side of Christ's return. Don't ask people to do too many different things, but do expect the word to go to work in those who receive it as God's word. Give people a starting place for obedience and next steps along the way so they can find themselves on the path of faith and run their own race, the race set before them.

Let's consider an example to crystallize what these undertakings involve. Suppose you are preaching 1 Timothy 4:1-16 and know from the context (1 Tim. 3:14-15) that this whole book is instruction for the church. You have studied the passage carefully and interrogated it. You conclude that this chapter is instruction concerning how to deal with false teaching so that the church may live up to its calling as the pillar and foundation of the truth. Your proposition is, 'Church leaders must deal with false teaching.' Your organizational sentence, anticipating the unspoken question, 'How do church leaders deal with false teaching?' is '1 Timothy 4:1-16 supplies *four steps* church leaders should follow in dealing with false teaching.' You articulate these four steps in the following outline.

I.   Expect it. (v. 1)
II.  Understand it. (vv. 2-5)
III. Explain it. (v. 6)
IV.  Counter it. (vv. 6-16)

---

[4]A helpful resource for exploring application further is Daniel Doriani, *Putting the Truth to Work: The Theory and Practice of Biblical Application* (Phillipsburg, N.J.: P & R Publishing, 2001).

Notice that each main point is a complete sentence with the subject (church leaders) understood. Stating the steps succinctly serves to underscore the verbs (*expect, understand, explain* and *counter*). They are *four steps that leaders should take* so they fulfill the expectations of the proposition and the organizational sentence. Each main point is anchored in the text of Scripture. Once you articulate your first point and read verse 1, it is more or less evident to the listener that we should expect false teaching precisely because, '*The Spirit clearly says that in the later times some will abandon the faith and follow deceiving spirits and things taught by demons.*' Further validation will not be necessary for some congregations; for others you may need to spell it out. In either event, you will need to *explain* how the Spirit says things, what the later times are, who these deceiving spirits are, and so forth. You might want to use some other images or examples that convey the truth that to be forewarned is to be forearmed. You help your listeners appreciate the love that God has for us – that he does not leave us vulnerable, apt to be blind-sided by false teaching. Application might include specific instances of false teaching that currently plague the church at large followed by a question such as, 'Are the elders of our church regularly scanning for these viruses every time they meet to pray for the church?'

Then you transition to the *second step* church leaders must take. You label it as such so your listeners can follow how your message is proceeding according to the plan promised in your organizational sentence. You say something like, '*Step two: understand it. Church leaders must understand false teaching. We find this in verses two to five.*' You read the verses and explain that these verses are really themselves an explanation of the kind of false teaching Paul has in mind. You point out that false teaching is mediated by false teachers who are hypocrites and liars with cauterized consciences. Their false teaching is made concrete and specific by citing two examples (marriage and diet) that have in common a faulty view of creation. You spell out God's good purposes for both these gifts and how he intends his people to receive them. Paul's explanation of the truth provides a context for and a definition of the error he is countering. This, by the way, is a great model of how to get below the surface of doctrinal error by looking for the faulty emphasis or what is neglected in the defective theology. You will continue to elaborate the data in the text to make the point that before church leaders can take the next step (*explaining* false teaching to the congregation) they themselves must understand it. You will want to drive this home by challenging church leaders to be Bible students and readers of good theology and church history so they can discern error.

You may then proceed to step three. 'Church leaders must *explain* false teaching.' This merely picks up the words of verse 6a, 'If you *point these things out* to the brothers, you will be a good minister of Jesus Christ.' You validate this by making a case that to lay these truths before your listeners is to explain false teaching, just as they have been explained to us as readers in the preceding verses. Now you emphasize not the explanation itself but the act of putting it before the congregation and the reward associated in the text with fulfilling that responsibility.

Once you have elaborated that idea, you move to the fourth step, recapitulating the first three with words such as, 'It is not enough merely to *expect* false teaching, or even to *understand* it as leaders, or even to *explain* its nature, origins, examples, and roots. We must also take a fourth step. We must *counter* it. You will see how Paul told Timothy to do this in verses 6-16.' These we now read and demonstrate from the text how countering false teaching requires both *articulating* the truth and *embodying* it. There is a lot in these verses that needs to be noted, but in this message to be preached to a whole congregation, you don't want to get bogged down in the details. All the care about associations, all the hard work and disciplines, the habits, the use of Scripture and exercise of gifts are so that our lives and teaching may agree. We become God's contemporary apologetic for the gospel when what we say and how we live both proclaim the word of God. Unless we do that as church leaders, parishioners will not learn to adorn the gospel and false teachings will grow like weeds in God's garden.

As I have tried to demonstrate, judicious repetition and careful transitions are crucial in making the point that the text is making. They are essential in oral discourse. Transitions sew the parts of the message together, demonstrating how they relate. They signal progress to your listeners and distinguish ideas, letting the listener know where you are in the outline. Transitions review what has been said and preview what will be said. They help tap back into the proposition. Transitions help repetition sound natural. You may use so called, 'knitting statements' like 'not only, but also ...', or 'if this is true, it follows that' or 'in the same way' or simply, 'next.' Transitions are a good time to draw in your listeners, engaging them in dialogue in which you supply the words that reflect what they should be thinking. This may be accomplished by stating a question raised by your exposition, that your listeners may be asking, such as, 'You may be saying to yourself, "Yes, but how can Paul say this, when just a few verses earlier he has said ... ?"' You then proceed to answer that question. Whatever you do, make these details serve the purpose for which you introduce them. Don't focus on them and feel free to leave things out if they distract you or your listeners. They are a means to an end; they help us let God's authentic voice be heard.

You may be saying to yourself, 'This is simply too much for the people to whom I preach. They don't have the stomach for this level of detail.' That may be true at the present, but they will never develop an appetite for the meat of the word if you do not serve it. You may be surprised how much people can digest and how far some will go beyond your own insights. If your teaching is faithful and clear it will commend itself to the consciences of your growing listeners. When your messages are solidly anchored to the text of Scripture and you make it plain that those links are valid, when you explain things winsomely with lots of word pictures, and speak everything to their hearts from yours for their good and God's glory, it will be *interesting*. Your concern is not to make this message from God palatable to those who are running from him, but to speak in the sight of God whose messenger you are (2 Cor. 4:2; 1 Thess. 2:5, 10). When you do that, he will do his part, using his word to speak to those present. Just as God's word takes various forms, your sermons will have different shapes. This one is only one of many, but it is one that maximizes the potential for faithfulness and clarity, when consecrated to the Lord every step of the way.

## 10. Write the Conclusion to the Message, including, as appropriate, a final prayer.

Don't leave your conclusion to the inspiration of the preaching moment. Craft your sermon's final words carefully. They will drive home the proposition by calling for the response it told us the text requires. You will have already applied the text piecemeal in most sermons. Now you must apply the whole. That means preaching the proposition, urging it upon your listeners, pleading with them in God's name to take seriously what God is saying to them today. Do this by gathering up the threads of the main points of your outline and showing again very briefly how they lead inescapably to the proposition and, in particular, to the response for which it calls. That is, say again how everything this passage teaches relates to your listeners.

This recapitulation can be deadly if it sounds like a mindless summary of what you have just told them. So consider putting an edge on it, showing how the sword of the Spirit cuts through to them. This may be done by recasting it just slightly, coming at the truth from a very slightly different angle that says the same thing but in a way that is different enough to make the response three dimensional and real. Often this is best done by a believable contemporary example of response to this text or a recent event that underscores the necessity of response. Such a story inspires them because it helps them see that the Holy Spirit can work this text into their lives too. Make sure it is brief and doesn't add new data to the teaching. It should focus their thoughts and not diffuse them.

End decisively. Some preachers praise the leave-them-hanging sort of conclusion because that pushes the listeners to a state of discomfort, a sort of disequilibrium that helps them to respond. We want people to respond, but in the final analysis, the gospel ends with an exclamation point, not ellipses marks. The sovereign glory of the Triune God is the certainty and finality that provides the foundation for, and hope of, any response we may offer up to him. We preach as those who are not relying ultimately on the responses of our listeners, but on the faithfulness of God to accomplish his purposes. That conviction needs to be reflected in the way we conclude our sermons. We end with a confident finality that makes response meaningful (cf. 1 Cor. 15:58).

This is one reason that ending with prayer, as long as it is not perfunctory, is appropriate. By ending in prayer, we commit the work of God's word to God himself, inviting him to use it to sanctify us and strengthen us for the obedience of faith. We thank him for what he is already doing and express our faith that he will continue to work. And we consecrate ourselves to the disciplines and steps of obedience for which the text calls. This prayer is not the occasion for wider supplication unless that is what the text has asked for.[5] Also, it should not recapitulate the points of the outline. Remember, prayer is speaking *to God*. Recapitulation for the benefit of our hearers should normally come earlier. Instead, we might pray

> Gracious Lord, please continue the good work you have begun in us until the day of Christ, working in us what is pleasing to you. Strengthen our wills by the work of your Holy Spirit that we might joyfully and gratefully do what you ask, to the honor of your name.

## 11. Write the Introduction to the Message.

This may seem like something you should have done before now, but in preparing to preach, this fits here even though when we actually preach the sermon it comes first. That is because until you know where the sermon is going, right down to the last words, you don't know the best way to start that journey. We need introductions because what we have to say is so important that we don't want people to miss it since they are still tuning in, debating whether or not to give us their attention, or have no idea of our subject and what difference it could possibly make to them. The good introduction achieves a dual goal. It invites our hearers' attention, first, by giving

---

[5] 1 Timothy 2:1-8, for instance, could very appropriately end in wide-ranging prayer as a specific first step of obedience.

them reasons for listening to the message, and second, it establishes our ethos or credibility as messengers. That is, it sets forth an important *subject* to be addressed by a credible *person*. Some preachers begin with a joke or other throw-away story, probably to establish rapport with the congregation. That is a valuable aim, but such an introduction does not usually promote interest in the subject or credibility. In the introduction we present ourselves as people to be taken seriously, and a joke does not help us in that task. Our goal is to establish our ethos as one to be listened to since our message is a word from God to be heeded.

Some of your listeners will be eager to listen. For them, too much introduction feels like a waste of precious time that could be spent probing the depths of the Bible. For such people, a simple statement of where you take up your study of God's word would be enough. Unfortunately, we can rarely assume that these people are in the majority. Others, perhaps most of your hearers, and every one of us at some time or another, need to be reminded that God has a word for us today. All sorts of devices can be used – human interest stories, provocative statements, news reports, cultural commentary, or searching questions. Whatever the means, the goal is to raise the issue that the text addresses. That is, we want to point to the problem, deficiency, need, challenge, or opportunity to which the Bible gives the solution, the provision, an answer, or a way forward.

Pointing to a human problem and biblical solution in our introduction does not mean that we foster a view of the Bible merely as an answer book to our questions or problems. Rather, our careful, theologically-informed study of the text in its context has discovered how this text fits into the drama and history of redemption. We have seen how the text expects us to respond to what God is doing. From the very beginning of the message, we want our listeners to have the confidence that the text does address their lives and an idea of the arena in which it does so. The introduction creates an expectation that the sermon intends to fulfill. It paints the backdrop against which we announce the proposition as good news. It puts on the listener's agenda the contemporary issue upon which the text sheds light. It stimulates the appetite for the meat of the word as

148 Prepared to Preach

summarized in the proposition. Therefore, we must craft an introduction that *introduces the proposition*, not the first main point, or even the text of Scripture. By introducing the proposition, you are already aiming for the response for which the text calls.

How do you do this in practice? As you meditate on the proposition, jot down whatever comes to mind that might bridge the gap between your listeners' worlds and the subject you will address. What might help them see themselves as responsible people living in the eternal reality that the Bible portrays? Some possibilities will rule themselves out almost immediately. One story is too long; another quotation is in poor taste; a third doesn't quite fit. A fourth has too many details, like a movie scene you have to describe in great detail to make your point. A fifth raises distracting peripheral issues that cloud things. Eventually a thought will occur that can be researched, if it is factual, or developed, if it comes from your own imagination. An introduction is like an on-ramp of an interstate highway; its purpose is to get you up to speed and in the flow of traffic quickly and safely. An introduction needs to get your listeners into a frame of mind to listen to the word of God actively and expectantly. Perhaps an illustration you rejected for the body of the sermon actually fits as an introduction or vice versa. Perhaps your introduction helps you address an unspoken objection.

Consider an example.

'On March 7, 2004 the *Chicago Tribune* printed a letter from Mr. Isaac Cohen. He wrote (in part),

'*The literal narrative of holy scripture, whether it's the Hebrew Bible, the New Testament or the Koran, is fraught with dangers. Though the three texts extol the virtues of charity, love and compassion, passages in all of them are brutal and doubt remains as to whether they were really inspired by God. They probably were written by men who in the context of their times, thought it wise to incorporate them in these texts and who by so doing hijack the religions for their own purposes. Wouldn't it be better for mankind to put aside these controversial passages, which have already caused so much misery, and instead concentrate on the beautiful ones extolling high ethical human values?'*

'Do you feel like Mr. Cohen does? Would we be better off to put aside brutal passages like those describing the death of Jesus on the cross? To address that honest question I invite you to look at our text for this morning ....'

If nothing comes to mind as you pray concerning an introduction, ask the Lord to help you *create* an imaginary story that achieves the purposes of an introduction – preparing listeners to hear you and to hear the message you bring from God. Introduce it as imaginary, and let it go to work bringing your listeners up to speed.

The introduction proper is not all you need to say to get people into the word. Here is a suggested sequence of introductory material with some explanatory comments. You may not include all these, but remember that, in oral discourse, you have to bring people along with you. They can't look back to the previous page to see the train of thought. This sequence works pretty well to bring people along. Repetition needs to be built in and you need to pace yourself. Here is what I would include:

**Pre-introduction**. This may be a word of thanks for the invitation to preach, or on occasion, some link to the worship just shared by all when it really requires some verbal acknowledgement. Often a pre-introduction is not necessary and can be omitted.

**Prayer.** Here you commit the message, yourself, and your listeners to God, inviting him to speak through you and submitting every heart and will to his word.

**Introduction proper**. This is the story, quotation, question, or statement that identifies the issue the text addresses.

### The proposition package consisting of:[2]
- **An introductory formula**, a phrase or sentence that alerts listeners to the proposition. For instance, 'My message today is really very simple.'
- **The proposition stated.** Say it just the way you have worked hard to express it. If you can't remember it yourself, keep

---

[2]I am indebted to Dr. Michael Bullmore for this concept and what follows by way of description.

editing for clarity and accuracy until you can. Say it from memory.

- **The proposition paraphrased or restated in a different way.** This gives people time to let it sink in or perhaps write the proposition in their notes.
- **The proposition restated verbatim.**

**Organizational sentence.**

**Words directing listeners to the text itself**. 'Please turn with me to Ephesians 1, verses 3-14. While you are turning . . .'

**A *brief* introduction to the text**, giving its historical and textual context and other pertinent information that must be heard before the text is read. *Sometimes* this will include clearing the ground culturally or theologically so your listeners know in what context you are reading this passage. For example, when your text is Ephesians 5:22-33, it makes sense to prepare listeners who might otherwise write these words off as barbaric chauvinism. When necessary, this also prepares people to listen not only to the text as you read it, but also to what you are going to say from it because you make it plain what you are *not* going to try to accomplish.

**Read the whole text** (unless it is a lengthy narrative of multiple chapters; in that case read portions). Read it so well that if you were called away and did not have the opportunity to preach, every listener would grasp its essential message, or at least begin to do so. I would recommend you do this even if the text has already been read earlier in the worship service (1 Tim. 4:13). Repetition is the mother of all learning.

**State and anchor first point,** and proceed to develop your outline.

You will develop your own habits, and each congregation will have its own expectations. Resist two temptations: on the one hand, *abruptness* where you say too little by way of introduction and catapult your listeners prematurely into the deep waters of the text, and on the other, *verbosity* where you say entirely too much and so delay getting into the text. The latter is the graver transgression because it leaves the impression that what *you* have to say about the Bible is more important than what the Bible itself has to say.

# 17

# Preparing to Deliver the Message

**12. Write out the Message in Detail in good Oral Style.**
Now we take all the parts we have developed – the introduction, proposition, organizational sentence, outline (complete with anchoring, validation, explanations, illustrations, and applications), and conclusion, and write them all out in order as we anticipate *saying* them. That is the key. We are not writing an essay, much less a research paper with footnotes. We are putting on paper what we plan to say aloud in the assembly of God's people. Reading each paragraph aloud as you write may help you hear weaknesses you would not otherwise see.

You may resist this step thinking it unnecessary. It will take time, and that always seems in short supply. I highly recommend it for the following reasons:

- It helps us choose our words carefully. If God cares enough to inspire every word of the Bible, we should care enough to write out each word of our sermons.

- It forces us to think about transitions. How do we get from organizational sentence to first main point? Answering that question on paper helps you when you get there in person.

- It helps us detect problems of flow and logic, infrequency, or unnecessary bunching of illustrations. Often, a solution to some structural weakness will occur to us as we write because we cannot proceed until we correct the difficulty.

- It gives us an idea of the length of the sermon. After some experience you will know that so many pages of your typescript normally translate into so many minutes in the pulpit.

I will always be grateful that John Stott challenged some of us as beginners to write out our sermons in full for the first ten years of ministry. It is a discipline I still practice after thirty years, and it has helped me serve listeners better than would otherwise have been the case. If you preach several times a week, consider writing out *one* of those sermons.

How do we actually write in good oral style?[1] Like most skills, improvement comes with practice and having good models. Since many of the sermons that make up the commentaries of the late James Montgomery Boice were also preached for radio audiences, they provide good examples of clarity, order, and economy of expression with just enough internal repetition. *Reader's Digest* developed its editorial strategy based on the thinking of Rudolf Flesch who researched and practiced clear writing in the middle years of the twentieth century. Reading *Reader's Digest*, or Flesch's books, will improve your style.[2] Use concrete, particular words, aim for simplicity, and avoid jargon. Make your speech colorful and interesting by using sensory language, descriptive, concrete nouns and strong verbs.

The true secret of clarity is more basic. Underneath clear writing is clear thinking. You have already taken the most important steps toward clarity of thought in the first eleven steps just outlined. If you are unclear about *what* you are going to say, *how* you say it won't be easy. Sometimes, the thoughts are clear enough, but you have developed some bad habits in expressing them. Learn to edit your own writing and recruit skilled help. This is worth the effort, because clear writing is not only the fruit of clear thinking; it is, for many of us, the root of it too. Our thinking becomes clearer only when we get it down on paper and see what needs cleaning up. All this takes time, so start early.

## 13. Reduce the Manuscript to Notes.

Some preachers take a manuscript with them into the pulpit and speak directly from it. They may serve in churches where this is

---

[1] G. Robert Jacks, *Just Say the Word* (Grand Rapids: Eerdmans, 1996), 92-93, summarizes how to write for the ear.

[2] Rudolf Flesch, *The Art of Plain Talk* (New York: Harper and Brothers, 1946), *The Art of Readable Writing* (New York: Harper and Brothers, 1949), and *The Art of Clear Thinking* (Harper and Brothers, 1951).

expected and normal and where to have less documentation in hand leaves the impression that they are unprepared or are 'winging it'. For others of us, the impression we make when toting a manuscript is more negative than positive. We seem bookish and out of touch, aloof and straitjacketed. If we are perceived to be reading our message, readers may conclude that we ourselves aren't really involved in it. After all, they reason, suitors don't read proposals of marriage, do they? The use of Teleprompters by newscasters and other public speakers leaves the (false) impression that anyone who can't look directly at the audience is not up to standard.

The drawbacks of speaking from a manuscript are not limited to audience perception. Eye contact is more difficult to maintain. The manuscript pages themselves can be a distraction if we shuffle them and an absolute menace if we get them out of order. At a minimum, they are one more item between the speaker and the listeners and, as such, they create unwanted distance. Manuscripts, even when colorfully highlighted, demand detailed attention. If we lose our place we usually have to find the very word where we were derailed in order to get back on track. Subtly, a manuscript can detract from the centrality of the word of God itself. I have seen too many student preachers read the text, place their Bible on a shelf in the pulpit and never refer directly to it again despite lots of praiseworthy biblical content in the manuscripts they proceed to use. Very few of these preachers have done that a second time!

On the plus side, manuscripts facilitate hard-won verbal precision. They may bolster the confidence of the neophyte preacher who need not wonder what to say next. In a way, they take the focus off the preacher and put it on the message. If you can use a manuscript without succumbing to the attendant difficulties, more power to you.

These benefits notwithstanding, I think preachers are better off with one of two other alternatives. The first and more ambitious is to memorize the message and preach it without notes. This is easier than you may have thought. Just memorize five or six five-minute talks and remember the order in which to give them. This strategy has the great advantage of forcing the preacher to make the message memorable! It also removes at least one barrier between you and the congregation, namely notes or manuscript. Potentially it removes a second barrier if it frees you to dispense with pulpit as well, but then you have to decide how to hold your Bible. Too often the one-hand, wrap-around, spine-breaking Bible hold and the hamstrung gesturing prove that the decision to eliminate the pulpit was not a good one. Having a pulpit on which to place the Bible shows respect for it and frees you to communicate with more of your body. The pulpit itself can be a reminder of the solidity and centrality of the word, and that the preacher is there to proclaim a message that is lasting and permanent.

There are two major drawbacks to preaching completely without notes. Some hearers, perhaps many, will leave worship with one dominant impression: 'That preacher is clever and capable!' 'Wow, he did all that without a single note!' Obviously this is not the change of consciousness we were hoping to achieve. That reaction may make us more self-conscious, worrying that we will forget something when we should be thinking about the congregation's need and God's wonderful provision of a word for them. The second major disadvantage is oversimplification. In order to memorize the message we may make it too simple. The methodology now dictates the content of the sermon instead of serving it. Anything we can't memorize we jettison, and sermons readily degenerate into a series of sound bites. Lengthier quotations and tight reasoning have a place in preaching, and it is a shame when a form of delivery rules them out. Having said that, some preachers have the gifts and graces to preach deeply yet humbly without manuscript or notes. The lasting impression when they do so is the glory of God. If you are one of these people give thanks to God and use the gifts he has given.

A second alternative to using a manuscript is to preach from the Bible, using notes, as few or as many as you need. This half-way house between manuscript and memorizing has the best of both worlds – freedom, but not at the expense of detail and depth. Try reducing your manuscript to lean notes that are just enough to remind you of the basic elements of the sermon (introduction, proposition, organizational sentence, outline and conclusion). Color-code the words, and write them on 8.5' x 5.5' card stock,[3] and secure the cards in a small loose leaf notebook with large rings.[4] This practice has several advantages. Card stock does not rattle or stick together like paper so pages can be turned easily without distraction. You can't get the pages out of order unless you manage to drop and break the notebook. You can more easily insert lately-developed illustrative material. If you lose your place, you can pick up the thread of your thought more readily because you are looking for a reminder, not looking for a specific word in look-alike typescript. You can vary print size to make the notes easy to read at a glance.

Whether you use a manuscript or notes, know what you are going to say well enough to be as free as possible. Think of the skilled conductor of a symphony orchestra who has the musical score on the lectern but certainly is not enslaved to it. Because he or she has mastered its contents, it functions now more as a general reminder of the location within the concert. I find that reducing my manuscript to notes clarifies my thinking even further, just as expanding my study notes did in creating the manuscript. Both steps serve clarity.

Whatever you do, use the technique that serves you best, as Dr. Robert Sanderson, former Regius Professor of Divinity at Oxford and a future bishop, learned the hard way:

> According to Walton, when the learned Dr. Henry Hammond tried to persuade Dr. Sanderson to trust himself to preach a short sermon without reading his manuscript so as to address a neighbouring village congregation with greater liveliness, directness, and freedom, the result was disastrous for both congregation and preacher. Hammond, who had Sanderson's sermon manuscript in his hand, saw that the latter was 'so lost as to the matter, especially the method, that he also

---

[3]Sometimes card stock in this size is hard to find and has to be specially printed. If you want to use a computer, a two-column, landscape format print-out, when folded in half and punched at the open (8.5 inch) side provides almost the same thickness as card stock and uses both front and back of each half page as it is now visible in your notebook. With a color printer, notes can be color coded so that you can pick up the thought at a glance more easily.

[4]Slightly smaller notebooks work too if pulpit space is limited.

became afraid for him, for it was [obvious] to many of that plain [congregation].' The upshot was that as they walked together back to Hammond's home, Dr. Sanderson said most eagerly, 'Good Doctor, give me my sermon and know, that neither you nor any man living shall ever persuade me to preach again without books [i.e., a manuscript].' A chagrined Dr. Hammond replied, 'Good Doctor, be not angry; for if I ever persuade you to preach again without book, I will give you leave to burn all the books that I am master of.'[3]

**14. Rehearse the Sermon Aloud until you are relatively free from your notes and can forget about yourself when preaching.** This step may seem to some like a counsel of impossibility. There just is not enough time. It may indeed be a luxury you cannot afford, especially if you preach several different messages a week. My counsel is to find a way to build this step into your schedule. For some preachers, practice is counterproductive because it *increases* self-consciousness rather than diminishing it. Having said that, the advantages to rehearsing – actually standing up and vocalizing your message – preferably in the place where you will preach it, outweigh the costs.

Practice will familiarize you with your notes and so increase your freedom from them. If you are an auditory learner, you may detect problems in the sermon that you failed to notice earlier because you did not *hear* them. You may find yourself *saying* better words than you *wrote* and culling unnecessary ones. Exercise may help you memorize your message, so that you don't have to think so much about your next word or phrase when you preach it. Practice will give you an opportunity to project your voice and will actually develop and condition the muscles necessary to do so. You will gain an opportunity to become aware of your posture, mannerisms, and other things that either enhance or detract from your preaching. Vocalizing may help you get emotionally involved with the message in a way that hasn't happened so far. This may be

[5]Horton Davies, *Worship and Theology in England: II. From Andrewes to Baxter and Fox, 1603–1690*, 141-42.

the time you actually preach this message to yourself, especially if meditating on it did not drive it home. Very likely this practice will send you back to your knees to pray that God would help you as you preach and would speak through you to the listeners.

If you are secure enough, you may choose to practice in front of a few well-chosen friends who will give you immediate feedback. The disadvantage of doing this is that you may feel some pressure for the message to be polished before it is or feel unable to stop mid-stream and start again. This process of preaching it to yourself can be painful, and some of us feel more comfortable suffering alone.

How many times do you need to practice? A single rehearsal may produce a sort of 'false positive,' a sense that you are ready when you are not. More than three practices may leave you jaded, tired and beyond the emotional peak, without the sense of freshness and excitement that the text brought when you first discovered or rediscovered its message. This is a particular danger when you have left preparation until too late and the rehearsals and the actual preaching come too close together. It is often better to prepare, practice, and then rest, allowing time before preaching so that you can come back to the message with a sense of freshness. Make it your goal to practice what you preach.

# 18

## Preparing Yourself to Deliver the Message

If you are being prepared by God, have prepared yourself to preach, and have prepared the message God has given you, you are prepared to preach! Yet all of us who preach, having done everything we know to do, still feel somehow unprepared. This is usually a good thing.[1] If we go into the pulpit confident in our preparation, we have not really understood the dynamics of preaching. It is better to feel like Isaiah in the temple (Isa. 6:1-13) or like Simon Peter, the professional fisherman, when Jesus told him where the fish were: 'Go away from me, Lord; I am a sinful man!' (Luke 5:8). Paul traces his own boldness to a very different source than self-confidence or thorough preparation. For one thing, he asks people to *pray* that he would speak boldly (Eph. 6:19-20). For another, he not only relies upon the Triune God but declares that reliance openly: 'Such confidence as this is ours through Christ before God. Not that we are competent in ourselves to claim *anything* for ourselves, but our competence comes from God. He has made us competent as ministers of the new covenant – not of the letter but of the Spirit; for the letter kills, but the Spirit gives life' (2 Cor. 3:4-6). When the Holy Spirit gives life through Christ, we are confident before God. That is the sort of confidence that really matters in preaching.

In 2 Corinthians 4, Paul describes how he maintains this confidence in the face of persecution, abandonment, and violent opposition. The secret is seeing time and eternity in light of the cross. By faith he grasps that the cross of Christ changes everything, including what we are thinking as we preach. What looks like failure now may actually be success in light of what God will do when a seed falls into the ground and dies. When death is at work in us,

---

[1] Learn to discern when the Spirit is prompting you to change something that is wrong or misleading. That does happen too!

God uses that to bring life in our hearers. It is this assurance, rooted in faith that the God who raised Jesus from the dead still raises the dead and will raise those in Christ on the last day, that enables Paul to preach. Beginning with a quotation from Psalm 116:10, Paul writes:

> It is written: 'I believed; therefore I have spoken.' With the same spirit of faith we also believe and therefore speak, because we know that the one who raised the Lord Jesus from the dead will also raise us with Jesus and present us with you in his presence. All this is for your benefit, so that the grace that is reaching more and more people may cause thanksgiving to overflow to the glory of God (2 Cor. 4:13-15).

Notice how this informed faith, this theology of the cross, takes the preacher's focus off self and places it squarely upon the benefit to the listeners and the glory of God. We can afford to neglect how we are treated by others in light of what we know God will ultimately do because we are in Christ. The most important final step in preparing to deliver the message is to exercise this faith. Until we forget ourselves, we are not ready to preach. Your ministry is important, but that is not where your focus should be. Our focus must be on the good of our listeners for the glory of God. This is not easy because we have just invested many hours getting ready. That sort of preparation biases us toward trusting in what *we* have done. Prayer along the way counters it, but does not completely eliminate it, if my own experience is anything to go by. We need to regain that eternal perspective that comes from fixing our eyes afresh on the unseen, recalling that although we are wasting away, God is building something eternal. He has stooped to let us share in that project as we die to self. When we take up our crosses his Holy Spirit goes to work opening blind eyes, granting new life, and establishing those who already believe. That is what we believe. That is why we preach.

Notice carefully that the conviction that God has made us for this very purpose does not lull us into inactivity. Instead, we are free to live for others whom we see differently and try to persuade in the name of Christ. We implore our listeners on Christ's behalf, urging them not to receive God's grace in vain (2 Cor. 5:11, 14, 16-17, 20; 6:1), precisely because God is making his appeal through us (2 Cor. 5:20). By faith we speak with confidence because it is not merely we who speak. We do not just have a word from God; God has a word to speak, and he does so through us when we speak the word he has given. Then the mixed reception we receive and the range of emotions we feel will embody the paradox of the cross and resurrection and actually commend the gospel and us as servants of God (2 Cor. 6:3-10). Our confidence comes not from what people say when we preach nor how we feel afterwards, but from what we know by faith.

When you have regained God's perspective, and are submitted to his work in and through you, *relax and rejoice.* Your performance is not the issue. You are free to feel and let your passion for the subject show because you are not preaching about yourself or trying to draw attention to yourself. Let the Spirit animate your speech, your face, and your movements. Let your sacrificial love for your hearers ring forth in your tone of voice. Be yourself. God gave this assignment *to you*, not someone else. God is going to work, and you have the privilege of being there when he does.

# Epilogue: Preparing to Preach
# Until Christ's Return[1]

We don't know when Jesus will return in power and great glory to judge and to save. It could be today; it could be in a hundred years. Every servant of the word must plan for both possibilities. That, I suspect, is why Matthew 24:36-51 is followed immediately by Matthew 25:1-12. In the first section, some people are caught off guard because the Lord returns *earlier* than they expected and he finds stewards beating fellow servants and getting drunk. In the second section, the Lord returns *later* than the foolish virgins expected. They drifted off to sleep, and last-minute preparation took them away from their rightful places of vigilant anticipation. These two temptations recur in every generation. Some who expect a later return neglect their present responsibility. Some who expect an earlier return neglect to prepare for a future responsibility. You and I don't want our ship of faith to run aground on either shoal. Happily, in both stories, there were some who were both wise and faithful. We need to imitate them. Though the metaphors seem to be mixed, our task is to be stewards and watchmen at the same time. We serve up the food God has given at the proper time as we keep watch. We don't neglect one to do the other. We live *in* the present, but not *for* the present. We don't know how long there will *be* a present, so we live each day as our last and each day as if there will be many days to follow. This gives our preaching a sanctified combination of urgency and foresight. I have preached to people who were not alive the following Sunday. I have also preached to people who listened almost every week for the nineteen years I

---

[1]I place this material here, at the end, because I hope you will grasp what goes into preparing *every* sermon before you undertake to plan *series* of sermons. If planning series of sermons is not your responsibility, you may choose to read this later when the need arises. On the other hand, it contains a partial review of what has been set forth and may be helpful to you now even if you are not thinking about planning.

served one church. Our challenge, in the light of what we confidently do *not* know, is to plan for both eventualities.

You may be mainly a guest preacher who responds to the invitations of others, using your gift and ministering the word according to their plan, not yours. Each message stands or falls alone. Or you may follow a widely used, prescribed plan, a lectionary where you have some choice about what passage to preach but not much. Most of us, however, at least share responsibility to think through how to provide more than a string of independent sermons. As elders, parachurch workers, conference speakers, visiting denominational leaders, seminary professors, and especially pastors, we owe it to the Lord and to our listeners to preach messages that together convey the pattern of sound doctrine entrusted to us. Churches need a balanced diet of the word, and that will not happen accidentally. It takes planning. Worship leaders need time to meditate prayerfully on the text to be preached so they can help fellow worshippers voice their praise and mutual exhortations with words that reinforce the message. Celebrations of the Lord's Supper and baptism are more meaningful when they respond to the word just preached than when they seem unrelated to it. All this takes planning, and planning presupposes good feedback from others, unhurried prayer, the conviction that God sovereignly guides, and a willingness to listen to God and others. Shared planning is often difficult for preachers because it implies shared control of the outcome and this can be threatening. Nevertheless, the church and you the preacher will benefit from it.

How do we go about it? Some very helpful resources are available and will repay your time in reading them.[2] Broadly speaking, there are two types of sermon series. First, the topical or thematic series is built around a biblical theme but draws the specific insights from passages that may come from anywhere in the Bible. Second, the expository type expounds a book of the

---

[2] James D. Berkley, *Leadership Handbook of Preaching and Worship* (Grand Rapids: Baker, 1992), 51-64. Stephen Nelson Rummage, *Planning Your Preaching: A Step-by-Step Guide for Developing a One-Year Preaching Calendar* (Grand Rapids: Kregel, 2002).

Bible, but may do this in more than one way. Let's consider the topical series first.

To plan a series of messages that are tied together by a biblical theme, the starting place is prayerfully to discern the topic God would have you develop. This process is a sanctified combination of knowing the people and their needs and being alert to what the Lord is underscoring as he speaks to you day by day from his word. As we discussed earlier, you will want to be aware of the general spiritual maturity of the sheep you shepherd and their specific needs. A pastoral conversation may bring to your attention some theological deficiency. For instance, a listener might confess knowing almost nothing about holiness, or wondering why baptism is important, or pondering the fact of hell and God's justice. When several such conversations point in the same direction, you might prioritize a series that speaks to that issue. This inclination may be reinforced if at the same time your own Bible study excites you about the same topic.

A second step is to study the subject using a concordance to look up all the passages that relate to this concept. Then use cross-reference tools to look for texts that may not use the words but deal with the subject. Then study the theme using other tools such as a good systematic theology, a Bible dictionary, or a Bible encyclopedia. Periodicals such as *Discipleship Journal* often have thoughtful, popular, thematic studies. As you study, note passages and themes that recur.

Third, limit the scope of your study by tentatively dividing the subject into narrower topics that naturally come under the heading of the larger subject. For instance, if you are studying fear, you might want to address such topics as fear of God, fear of man, recurrent fears, justifiable fears, or the fear of death. You may do this on the basis of subtopics that occur to you or with reference to passages that clearly address a subtopic. If you do the latter, you are well on the way to the fourth step. That step is to link each topic with one Bible passage that addresses it in a balanced way, or with a few texts that do so. Each text will provide the basis for a sermon. Fifth, develop each of these messages as we have outlined in Part Four, doing sufficient preliminary study to assure yourself that you have rightly discerned that the text is actually teaching the subject you say it is, or at least validly touches upon it. Make sure that there is enough in the text or texts to cover fairly the subtopic and for the message to stand on its own.

As you may readily deduce, this is no small task and requires a good deal of work well in advance of publicizing the series. Do not underestimate this. I know one very able preacher who had to abandon a series after a few weeks because he had not planned carefully enough. The series he had planned on the judges would be too repetitive because he anticipated one sermon per judge. What he failed to notice was that the theme of the book of Judges is recurrent, and all the examples make a similar point reinforcing it by repetition and building a bridge from Joshua to the monarchy. More careful study would have freed him to make the text's point, to employ judicious repetition, and to select a few *representative examples* of the judges instead of taking a week to explore each of them.

Another approach, which I recommend for the bulk of your ministry of the word, is to preach series of messages from individual books of the Bible. I offer nine reasons for making this your usual way of ministering the word.

1. The Bible was given to us as 'books' and collections of books, and not as verses or chapters. Although every word is inspired, we don't preach individual words. We preach larger units of text so that the context can help us understand what it is saying.

2. It takes more than one message to get the point. The natural use of repetition helps us solidify *this week* what *last week's* contiguous passage was teaching. When we preach consecutively through the Bible our listeners hear messages that cluster around the themes that were significant for the original hearers and therefore were focused toward specific responses. The messages build on one another. Biblical authors like Paul are allowed to develop their arguments carefully in our hearing even when they extend beyond the borders of a single preaching portion.

3. The preacher does not have to waste time every week wondering what to preach on Sunday. He does have to plan, but that involves the fruitful submission to a book of the Bible.

4. The congregation is more likely to understand *today's* text in its context when they have just recently heard a careful exposition of that very context. Less time is needed in the sermon itself to introduce the passage and place it in literary and historical context.

5. The congregation will not only learn what the passage before them is teaching, they will learn week by week how to interpret Scripture in its context. The preacher demonstrates sound methodology as well as teaching sound doctrine. This, in my view, is one of the most important reasons for careful, consecutive exposition of Scripture. The church must be filled not only with people who understand the Bible and live it, but with those who understand how to get sound doctrine from the Bible. They will be far less susceptible to the wiles of the devil, because like their Lord they know how to rightly handle the word when the enemy misapplies it.

6. The pastor is less likely to teach pet ideas or react to current fads, crises, or pressures. He is significantly more likely to teach the whole counsel of God, achieving variety by capitalizing on the variety built into the literature of the canon, and achieving balance by not neglecting any part of it.

7. Difficult subjects *can* be dealt with in a way that does not raise the question, 'Why is the pastor speaking about this?' When you come to Matthew 19 you deal with divorce without every divorced person present feeling targeted. Conversely, challenging subjects and difficult passages *must* be handled. You simply cannot skip the subject of homosexuality in Romans 1 or of giving in 2 Corinthians 8–9 despite internal or external pressures you may feel to do so.

8. The pastor-teacher is obliged to do a thorough study of the text of Scripture that refreshes his own soul and encourages feeding on the text as opposed to hunting for a text that communicates an already-existing idea the preacher thinks needs to be heard. A lifetime of

careful study of Scripture in a balanced, respectful, submissive way is a recipe for spiritual maturity. You can tell the difference between the sixty-year-old man who disciplined himself over the years to eat a balanced diet and his contemporary who mainly frequented one fast-food restaurant after another ordering only what was on special that day.

9. This approach lends itself most readily to congregational involvement in the sermon series. With a little help, individuals can plan their devotional reading from the announced text. Families can use supplementary materials to prepare their children to profit from Sunday's sermon. Small group Bible studies can preview or review the message. The church library can feature the best commentaries on the Bible book being studied.

For these reasons, I hope you will make consecutive exposition of Bible books your default setting in sermon planning. It won't be the *only* way you minister the word in public, but it will be the foundational way.

Having said that, keep in mind that not all series based on books of the Bible are the same, because not all books of the Bible are the same. Some series are straightforward *consecutive expositions* of the book. The preacher deals with each section of the book in order of appearance, not skipping or slighting any. The goal is to explain and apply the teaching of the book, no more and no less. The expositor may take larger or smaller portions of the text depending upon various factors, but the text itself sets the agenda.

On the other hand, a *thematic* series from a book involves drawing out the teaching of the book, faithfully articulating its theology, major themes, and application but not necessarily preaching every passage. The book itself still sets the agenda, but not every passage is expounded. For example, a series from Jeremiah could proceed in this fashion because it is an anthology of prophecies and Jeremiah's reflections upon them. Its chronology is not obvious and the oracles seem to be more thematic than sequential. The goal of this sort of preaching plan is to shorten the series without being unfair to the reasons the book of Jeremiah is in the Bible.

A third sort of sermon series from a Bible book could be called a *subject* series.[3] It selects from many possible subjects taught in a single Bible book one that the preacher thinks need to be preached now to the congregation. So, for instance, you could preach on the glory of God in Isaiah and have plenty of material but neither exhaust the subject of God's glory (in the whole canon) nor cover the whole of Isaiah's prophecy. This is the least satisfying way to treat a book, but it may have a place when time is limited as on a weekend retreat or for an advent series or some other time when the subject matter needs to be limited and when you want to have people focus on a single book of the Bible.

A fourth way is to *expound in detail part* of a Bible book. You might preach the Sermon on the Mount from Matthew 5–7, or how Israel and the nations relate from Romans 9–11. On another occasion, you might expound the letters to the seven churches from Revelation.

How do you decide which approach to take at any point in time? There are various factors to consider, some not unlike those that help you decide individual texts to preach.

### Factors relating to the congregation

- Do your listeners mainly need evangelizing or establishing? Do most need rebuking and correcting, or training and reminding?
- Are there manifest needs of the church or group *as a whole* that need to be addressed?
- How receptive are your listeners to the word of God? They may need milk at this point and not meat (1 Pet. 2:1-3; Heb. 5:12). Do they need you to go back over basic teachings? (Heb. 5:11-14).
- How long a message can they tolerate? Expounding a passage properly takes time and you may need to take the text in smaller bites until they grow in their ability to digest it.

---

[3]'Topical' might seem the obvious word here, but homileticians usually employ that word to refer to sermons that draw ideas from any passage as long as the content concerns the topic set by the preacher.

- What is the age range and maturity level represented among your hearers? The challenges of preaching increase with the range. Clarity and concreteness with plenty of word pictures will help listeners at every point on the spectrum. However, if the congregation is mainly young and relatively immature, you will begin with basic teaching that can be built upon when hearers are largely older and more mature.

- What is the educational level of most of the listeners? Greater education does not give you license to be abstract or stilted, or to ignore the less educated who may be present. It may allow you to assume some listening and note-taking skills. Education certainly should not be equated in your mind with intelligence or spiritual vitality.

- Will most of your listeners have studied or at least read the text in preparation for the sermon? This depends largely on what structures the church has in place to foster such practices. You can't assume that every listener will have taken advantage of such opportunities, but those who have are more likely to be ready to get down to responding to the text instead of merely grasping its teaching.

## Factors relating to you, the preacher

- How much experience and maturity do you have? Don't pursue a plan that will require you to make judgments about content and intent that are beyond your current abilities. Seasoned preachers can do faithful and valuable thematic studies that younger preachers should not attempt until they can discern the forest from the trees.

- What is your level of knowledge? Ideally you won't be entrusted with preaching until you know enough to do so, but some are thrust into pastoral leadership without much or any background in the church. They don't have much ballast on board and their formal training has supplied good tools but these hardly have the paint worn off them. Select a plan that will help you supplement and integrate your own Bible knowledge and put it into a coherent theological pattern. If you have a lot of theological knowledge, allow yourself time to bring that to bear on each text and show your listeners valid connections between the ideas taught in this passage and the larger pattern of sound doctrine.

• What is your level of pastoral wisdom? The more you have, the more truth and wisdom you will see in any text of Scripture. Sermons will have fuller application and therefore be longer. Consequently, you will need to allow enough time for each one and take the whole book in smaller bites.

• How skilled are you at being selective? Newly trained preachers tend to say too much in each sermon. Don't assume you have to share all you know whenever you preach, even if that is theoretically possible!

## Factors relating to the calendar

• At a season when many parishioners are on vacation, plan for a series that makes sense even if you miss a few Sundays.

• At times of new beginnings like the beginning of the school year, plan a series that capitalizes on the eagerness to get to work that the calendar underscores.

• Use advent or lent to tap into cultural openness to certain sorts of messages.

## Factors relating to the larger plan of preaching: achieving balance

• Each series should be short enough so as not to seem interminable. This means that you are always planning the next few series and have to consider how they fit together.

• If you have not preached the Old Testament (or New) for a while, address that imbalance.

• If you have been in the epistles, preach something from a narrative section.

- If you have been expounding the oracles of a prophet, consider following up with gospel fulfillment.

- If you have been preaching texts that are mainly applicable individually, preach something that emphasizes the need for corporate response. For instance, if you have been preaching from Proverbs on the power of words and exhorting people to use them carefully, you might preach from Ephesians or one of the Pastoral Epistles where corporate responsibility is more prominent.

- If you have been preaching some doctrinal, tightly-reasoned book like Romans, you might expound some Psalms that move us to obedience by tapping in to our feelings as well as shaping our thoughts.

- If you have been preaching sweeping messages from texts that emphasize big concepts like God's sovereignty or his plan for history, consider a series that is more microscopic, such as the Beatitudes or the fruit of the Spirit.

- If you are completing an exceptionally long series, plan the next one to be short.

How do you actually decide what book of the Bible to preach? First and always, you pray. Ask God to lead you to a book of the Bible and an approach to it that is healthy for the church and for you. Ask him to incline your heart to a book and to excite you about it and about preaching it. This seems to happen when we take time. A quiet day, a personal retreat, or even a family vacation can sometimes provide the space where God gets your ear. It may happen in the context of your own daily devotional study. If in your disciplined reading of the whole Bible one book seems to jump off the page and you find yourself underlining parts you have never noticed before, it may be because God wants to speak from that book to the congregation you serve. When a possible candidate emerges, take into account the factors just reviewed, then invite feedback from others who might by their enthusiasm help confirm God's leading or, by their misgivings, keep you prayerfully searching.

Once you have settled on a book, some important steps need to be taken to transform the idea of preaching a certain book into a sermon series from it. I would encourage you to begin to take these steps several months in advance with the actual time needed depending upon your setting, how much administrative help you have, and your own work habits.

1.  Prayerfully read and re-read the Bible book until its dominant themes emerge. It may help to make a list of the questions this book addresses and raises.

2.  Think of the congregation who will hear this series and begin to connect the dominant themes to their evident needs.

3.  Consult authorities, friends, librarians, and others to determine which commentaries to use, buy, borrow, or otherwise consult. Using interlibrary loan can save money in the short run and help you decide if a commentary is worth buying.

4.  Read the introductions to these commentaries to review or learn the background, theology, authorship, occasion, and other things about the book.

5.  Explore several ways of dividing the book into preaching portions, including consecutive exposition, thematic, and topical treatments. At this point you should develop a rough idea of how many preaching portions there are and, therefore, how many sermons will be required to do justice to the text.

6.  Match these proposed preaching portions with calendar dates on a worksheet that includes other events in the life of the church that need to be taken into account. For example, celebrations of the Lord's Supper, baptisms, infant dedications, and days for emphasising missions might be times when you take a smaller portion or interrupt the series.

7.  Once you have a tentative schedule, read each passage to summarize its thrust for your worksheet and to reassure yourself that it does not cover too much or too little ground. You may decide to preach more than one message from the same paragraph if it raises issues of particular importance to the

congregation. Review this list of summaries together with what you have learned from commentary introductions and draft a series title.

8.  Distribute this draft schedule (clearly marked as such) to worship planners, ministry colleagues, church secretaries, and others, inviting their feedback. They may know something about the schedule you have forgotten or spot an error in your allocation of passages to dates. Make necessary revisions and go to print with a final version which goes to ministry leaders. This will include the subject of each message, but should make it plain that closer to the preaching date the text itself may call for revision of the actual title of the sermon. Just before the series begins, publish the schedule for the congregation so they can anticipate in more detail what is ahead.

9.  Start a file on each message. As you read and meditate on the text, include in the file such things as possible hymns and songs that come to mind, illustrations, insights, other ideas, and whatever else is useful to you as you get down to serious study of each text.

10. Continue to read the whole book as often as you can in the months preceding your exposition of it, using the files you have created for insights and questions.

11. Read theologies and popular books that parallel the subject matter of the biblical book, filing the gleanings of your study.

12. Begin the detailed study of the text as outlined in Part Four early enough that you leave yourself time to let its truth sink in and work itself out.

As steps like these become good habits, they will become second nature. Use them to God's glory until Christ returns.

'Amen. Come, Lord Jesus' (Rev. 22:20).

# Select Bibliography

Adam, Peter. *Hearing God's Words: Exploring Biblical Spirituality*. Downers Grove: Inter-Varsity Press, 2004.

Adam, Peter. *Speaking God's Words: A Practical Theology of Expository Preaching*. Downers Grove: Inter-Varsity Press, 1996.

Alexander, James W. *Thoughts on Preaching*. Oxford: University Printing House, 1988.

Azurdia, Arturo G. III. *Spirit Empowered Preaching: The Vitality of the Holy Spirit in Preaching*. Fearn, Scotland : Christian Focus, 1998.

Blomberg, Craig L. *Preaching the Parables: From Responsible Interpretation to Powerful Proclamation*. Grand Rapids: Baker Academic, 2004.

Borgman, Brian. *My Heart For Thy Cause: Albert N. Martin's Theology of Preaching*. Fearn, Scotland: Christian Focus, 2002.

Bridges, Charles. *The Christian Ministry with An Inquiry into the Causes of its Inefficiency*. Carlisle, PA: Banner of Truth, 1997.

Bryson, Harold T. *Expository Preaching: The Art of Preaching Through a Book of the Bible*. Nashville: Broadman & Holman, 1995.

Capill, Murray A. *Preaching with Spiritual Vigour*. Fearn, Scotland: Christian Focus, 2003.

Carrick, John. *The Imperative of Preaching: A Theology of Sacred Rhetoric*. Cambridge: Cambridge University Press, 1982.

Chapell, Bryan. *Christ-Centered Preaching: Redeeming the Expository* Sermon. 2nd ed., Grand Rapids: Baker Books, 2005.

Chapell, Bryan. *Preach with Power*. Wheaton: Crossway, 2001.

Clowney, Edmund P. *Preaching Christ in All of Scripture*. Wheaton: Crossway Books, 2003.

Doriani, Daniel M. *Putting the Truth to Work: The Theory and Practice of Biblical Application*. Phillipsburg, New Jersey: P&R Publishing, 2001.

Ellsworth, Wilbur. *The Power of Speaking God's Word*. Fearn, Scotland: Christian Focus, 2000.

Eswine, Zack. *Kindled Fire: How the Methods of C.H. Spurgeon can help your Preaching*. Fearn, Scotland: Christian Focus, 2006

Fee, Gordon D. and Douglas Stuart. *How to Read the Bible Book by Book*. Grand Rapids: Zondervan, 2002.

Fee, Gordon D. and Douglas Stuart. *How to Read the Bible For All Its Worth*. Grand Rapids: Zondervan, 1993.

Gibson, Scott M. *Preaching the Old Testament*. Grand Rapids: Baker, 2006

Goldsworthy, Graeme. *Preaching the Whole Bible as Christian Scripture: The Application of Biblical Theology to Expository Preaching*. Grand Rapids: Eerdmans, 2000.

Green, Christopher and David Jackman. *When God's Voice is Heard: The Power of Preaching*. Leicester: Inter-Varsity, 1995.

Greidanus, Sidney. *The Modern Preacher and the Ancient Text: Interpreting and Preaching Biblical Literature*. Grand Rapids: Eerdmans, 1988.

Greidanus, Sidney. *Preaching Christ from the Old Testament: A Contemporary Hermeneutical Method*. Grand Rapids: Eerdmans, 1999.

Hughes, Jack. *Expository Preaching with Word Pictures*. Fearn, Scotland: Christian Focus, 2001.

Johnson, Darrell W., *The Glory of Preaching: Participating in God's Transformation of the World*. Downers Grove: IVP Academic, 2009.

Johnson, Dennis E. *Him We Proclaim: Preaching Christ from All the Scriptures*. Phillipsburg, New Jersey: P & R Publishing, 2007.

Kaiser, Walter C. Jr. *Preaching and Teaching from the Old Testament*. Grand Rapids: Baker Academic, 2003.

Liefeld, Walter L. *From Text to Sermon: New Testament Exposition*. Grand Rapids: Zondervan, 1984.

Lloyd-Jones, D. Martyn. *Preaching and Preachers*. London: Hodder and Stoughton, 1976.

Long, Thomas G. *Preaching and the Literary Forms of the Bible*. Philadelphia: Fortress, 1989.

Mathews, Alice P. *Preaching That Speaks to Women*. Grand Rapids: Baker Academic, 2003.

Mathewson, Steven D. *The Art of Preaching Old Testament Narrative*. Grand Rapids: Baker Academic, 2002.

McCann, J. Clinton, Jr. and James C. Howell. *Preaching the Psalms*. Nashville: Abingdon Press, 2001.

McLean, Max and Warren Bird, *Unleashing the Word: Rediscovering the Public Reading of Scripture*, Grand Rapids: Zondervan.

Osborne, Grant R. *The Hermeneutical Spiral: a Comprehensive Introduction to Biblical Interpretation*. 2nd ed., Downers Grove: 2006.

Piper, John. *The Supremacy of God in Preaching*. 2nd ed., Grand Rapids: Baker, 2004.

Quicke, Michael J. *360-degree Preaching: Hearing, Speaking and Living the Word*. Grand Rapids: Baker Academic, 2003.

Richard, Ramesh. *Preparing Expository Sermons: A Seven-Step Method for Biblical Preaching*. Grand Rapids: Baker, 2001.

Robinson, Haddon W. *Biblical Preaching,* 2nd ed. Grand Rapids: Baker Academic, 2001.

Robinson, Haddon W. and Torrey W. Robinson. *It's All in How You Tell It: Preaching First-Person Expository Messages*. Grand Rapids: Baker, 2003.

Robinson, Haddon and Craig Brian Larson, eds. *The Art and Craft of Biblical Preaching: A Comprehensive Resource for Today's Communicators*. Grand Rapids: Zondervan, 2006.

Ryken, Leland, James C. Wilhoit and Tremper Longman III, eds. *Dictionary of Biblical Imagery*. Downers Grove: InterVarsity Press, 1998.

Sargent, Tony. *The Sacred Anointing: The Preaching of Dr. Martyn Lloyd-Jones*. Wheaton: Crossway, 1994.

Smith, Steven W., *Dying to Preach: Embracing the Cross in the Pulpit*. Grand Rapids: Kregel, 2009.

Stewart, James S. *Heralds of God*. Grand Rapids: Baker, 1979.

Stott, John R.W. *The Preacher's Portrait: Some New Testament Word Studies*. Grand Rapids: Eerdmans, 1961.

Thompson, James W. *Preaching Like Paul*. Louisville, Kentucky: Westminster John Knox Press, 2001.

Webster, Douglas D., *Text Messaging: a Conversation on Preaching*, Toronto: Clements, 2010.